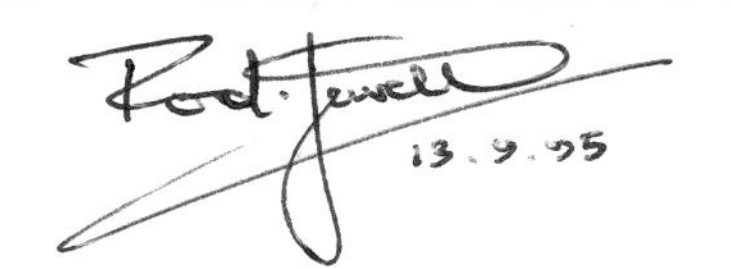

C000172618

Images of

Belper & Ambergate

THE ROD JEWELL COLLECTION

Images of Belper & Ambergate

Breedon Books
Publishing Company
Derby

First published in Great Britain by
The Breedon Books Publishing Company Limited
44 Friar Gate, Derby, DE1 1DA
1995

Acknowledgements

The author would like to thank the many people who found time to talk to him and release their local knowledge. Janet & Edward Burdekin, Gladys Blount, Dennis Hough, Mrs McFarlane, John Fletcher, Bert & Peggy Taylor, Cuth Wain, Betty Robinson, Janice & Daniel O'Keefe, Andrew Knighton, George Taylor, Ray Walters, Cheryl & Roy Marchant, Brian Key, Belper Historical Society, Bill Brocklehurst, Tom Lebeter Gibson, Gordon Lee, Chris Balls, Jackie Woodward, John West, Audrey Clutterbuck, Rachael Parsons.

Dedicated to
Julie & Minnie
and Ambergate Friends

ISBN 1 85983 029 3

Printed and bound by Butler & Tanner, Frome, Somerset.
Jackets printed by Premier Print, Nottingham.

Contents

Belper **6**

Introduction
The Strutt Family and Mills
Strutt's Farms
View from Bridge Hill
Bridge Foot and Wyver Lane
Belper River Gardens
Places of Worship
The Parks
Bridge Street and Chapel Street
Babbington Hospital
Belper Isolation Hospital
King Street
The Market Place and The Butts
Belper Schools and Colleges
The Military
Belper Houses
Sport
Social History
Openwoodgate

Ambergate **118**

Introduction
The Railway at Ambergate
The Ambergate Lime Works
The Aquaducts and Canal
Stevenson's Dye Works
Ambergate Wire Works and The Johnson Family
Oakhurst
The Canal
Churches
Halfpenny Toll Bridge
Holly Dene
The Woods
Military
Passing Through Ambergate
The Gas Plant
Derby Road
General Views of Ambergate
The Post Offices
The Ambergate Show
Buckland Hollow
Annals

Belper Introduction

The Belper Township

The illustration opposite was taken from an early playing card game. This late Victorian first series was an early round game called 'The Counties of England' issued *c.*1901 and cost 1s 6d. The similar second series was advertised as a 'Geographical Game', issued *c.*1910.

Both show the population of Belper at that time and also illustrate Belper's former staple trades of nailmaking and cotton/silk spinning. Belper has been a relatively large town now for well over 200 years. The 1811 census confirmed Belper as Derbyshire's second largest town and it was considered to be the third largest in 1840. The township in 1841 contained 1,830 inhabitated houses with 9,885 inhabitants (approximately an average of five people per house). Some of the known census figures are listed here:-

1740 - 532
1801 - 4,500
1811 - 5,635
1821 - 7,235
1831 - 8,000
1841 - 9,885
1851 - 10,082
1881 - 9,875
1891 - 10,420
1901 - 10,934
1911 - 11,643
1921 - 12,324
1931 - 13,023

Belper's Growth/History

Nailmaking had been established on a small scale since *c.*1260 the principal demand being for horsenails. However as the Strutt's Cotton Industry grew so did the Belper Nail Industry. By 1846 over 650 people were employed in nailmaking with just under 200 nailshops in existence. This figure had increased to 800 by 1857 but competition from machine made nails saw a rapid decline in the number of Belper nailers and by the turn of the century the industry was all but lost.

The real growth in Belper's township was largely due to the building of Strutt's cotton spinning mills from 1776 through to 1813. In 1789 the Belper Mills employed 600 workers and within the next 13 years this had over doubled to 1,300. By 1820 the Strutts employed 1,700, and by 1833 the number of workers were 2,000. By 1832 the firm of Ward, Brettle & Ward had become the largest hosiery firm in the country and at their highest point employed over 1,000. Other factors in Belper's growth were the building of the Midland Railway from 1836-1840 and the early Iron Foundries of the Smedley Brothers.

The ancient name for Belper was Beaupoire or Belle Piere signifying Fair Stone from the whiteness of the stone in its quarries. Although the Doomsday Book recorded it as Bradelei in 1086. The first Lords of the Manor were the De Ferrers. Edmund Crouchback, the Earl of Lancaster and second son of Henry III, later acquired the Manor of Belper and a hunting seat to which he gave the name Beau Repaire (meaning Beautiful Retreat), eventually that being corrupted to 'Belper'. After the final enclosure act of 1634 the Manor and 72 acres of the wooded former deer park were sold to the Jodrell family who were Duffield landowners and thus became part of the Duffield Manor.

Belper should really be renamed Strutt Town for the town has grown and consistently benefited from the Strutt family gifts and its benevolence for just under 150 years. (See Appendix A for list of Strutt family achievements/influence.)

However the purpose of this book is not to re-tell the ancient history of Belper, but rather to share with others the magnificent topographical and social history scenes recorded by Belper's own early photographers during the period from 1887 through to the 1930s.

The Belper Photographers: Bygone Belper has been preserved through the prolific output of its local photographers and the following were recorded:-

Kelly's 1888 Directory
George Julian Jackson – The Butts.
William Samuel Bowler – Bridge Street

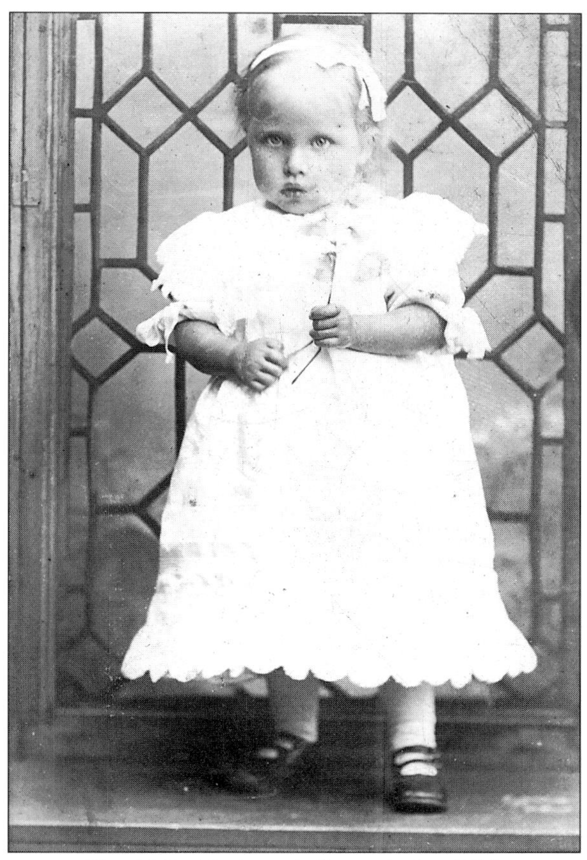
Harold Burkinshaw studio portrait, *c.*1910.

Jacob Schmidt – New Road and Campbell Street.
Norman Jones McAuslan – Brook Side/New Road.

Bulmer's 1895 Directory
George Julian Jackson – The Butts.
William Samuel Bowler – Bridge Street.
Fredrick Holbrook – Albert Street.
John William Wayne – New Road.

Kelly's 1912 Directory
George Julian Jackson – The Butts.
William Samuel Bowler – Bridge Street
Fredrick Holbrook – now George Street (and New Road)
Harold Burkinshaw – New Road (and King Street)
Edward William Smith – Chapel Street

Portrait by Norman Jones McAuslan of New Road.

Portrait by Midland Photographic Company, Belper.

Studio portrait by Harold Burkinshaw of New Road/King Street.

Misses E. & G.Wayne - now Chapel Street (and King Street)

Kelly's 1928 Directory
Edward E. Bowler - 110 Bridge Street
Mrs Mary Holbrook - now Green Lane
Walter Beardhall - 16 King Street
William Beckwith - Bridge Street

Other photographers include T.B.Mellor of Nottingham Road and The Midland Photographic Company Belper both of which were not listed in the aforementioned Directories. Norman McAuslan was listed in 1888 as a shopkeeper on Brookside whilst William Samuel Bowler kept a chemists shop on Bridge Street and also sold photographic apparatus. Belper's early notable photographers were George Julian Jackson and

Harold Burkinshaw's shop on the corner of King Street and Chapel Street.

Fredrick Holbrook both of whom operated as photographers prior to the introduction of the popular picture post-card era. However Belper's most prolific and important photographer was Harold Burkinshaw who commenced his contributions *c.*1905 from his premises on New Road. This photograph (above) shows Burkinshaw's other premises on the corner of King Street and Chapel Street. The small wooden shop had examples of his fine work on display in the window and in cabinets outside. (The shop exists today as an Estate Agents office).

Harold Burkinshaw commenced his work at the beginning of the 'Golden Age' of the picture post.

Both Fredrick Holbrook and Harold Burkinshaw also produced fine Edwardian cabinet/carte-de-visit style studio portrait photographs. But they along with the others were soon producing important historical documents in the form of rare images on picture post-cards. The following scenes include nearly 200

Midland Photographic Co, Belper, studio portrait.

previously unpublished illustrations once again to stir the memories of the Belepr people and those interested in its post.

The Strutt Chronicles (Appendix 'A')

1758 Jedediah Strutt invented the Derby Rib machine.
1776 Strutts First Timber framed south cotton mill erected. Original weir built.
1777 Strutts bought ironworks/forges at Makeney and Milford.
1786 The timber framed North Mill built.
1786 Jedediah instituted a Sunday School in the top storey of the North Mill.
1788 Jedediah had the Unitarian Chapel built in Field Row off Green Lane.
1790 Milford Bridge built over the Derwent.
1793 Strutts commenced building mill workers houses in Short Row then Long Row.
1794 Bridge Hill House built for George Benson Strutt.
1795 The mill overseers houses built on the Clusters. Gangway link built across the Ashbourne Road.
1796 The West Mill was completed.
1797 The Horseshoe Weir was built.
1803 North Mill destroyed by fire but rebuilt as iron framed mill by William Strutt.
1808 The six-storey Reeling Mill built.
1809 The Junction Mill built linking the West and Reeling Mills.
1810 Jedediah II (George Benson Strutt's son) had Green Hall built.
1812 Old South Mill demolished and new five storey south mill built.
Strutts Farms of Wyver, Crossroads and Moscow in operation to feed mill workers.
1813 Round Mill built and in production by 1816.
1818 Long Row Lancastrian schools built by William and Joseph Strutt.
1829 George Henry Strutt (son of Jedediah II) laid foundation stone to Matthew Smith's almshouses on the Butts.
1832 Princess Victoria visited Strutts Mills.
Strutts' private bridge built over King Street linking Green Hall & Paddock Garden.
1840 George Benson Strutt provided land for a new workhouse.
1854 The North Mill chimney built.
1856 Edward Strutt (William's son) became Lord Belper
1867 Strutt's King Street bridge demolished.
1870 George Henry Strutt took over the Matthew Smith Charity.
1881 Market Place paved by George Henry Strutt.
1884 George Herbert Strutt elected top of the poll in new County Council.
Open-air swimming baths opened and presented to Belper by George Herbert Strutt.
1886 Reading room at St John's Road built by George Henry Strutt.
1888 Conservative Club built in Campbell Street on land donated by George Herbert Strutt.
1890 George Herbert Strutt financed conversion of Union Workhouse into a hospital. (Babbington)
1895 George Henry offered interest-free loan of £11,700 to buy out the poorly-run local water company.
1896 Belper UDC formed.
1898 The Jubilee Clock Tower erected by George Herbert Strutt in honour of Queen Victoria's Jubilee.
1901 George Herbert fulfils his fathers wish and formally transfers deeds for new water pumping works and

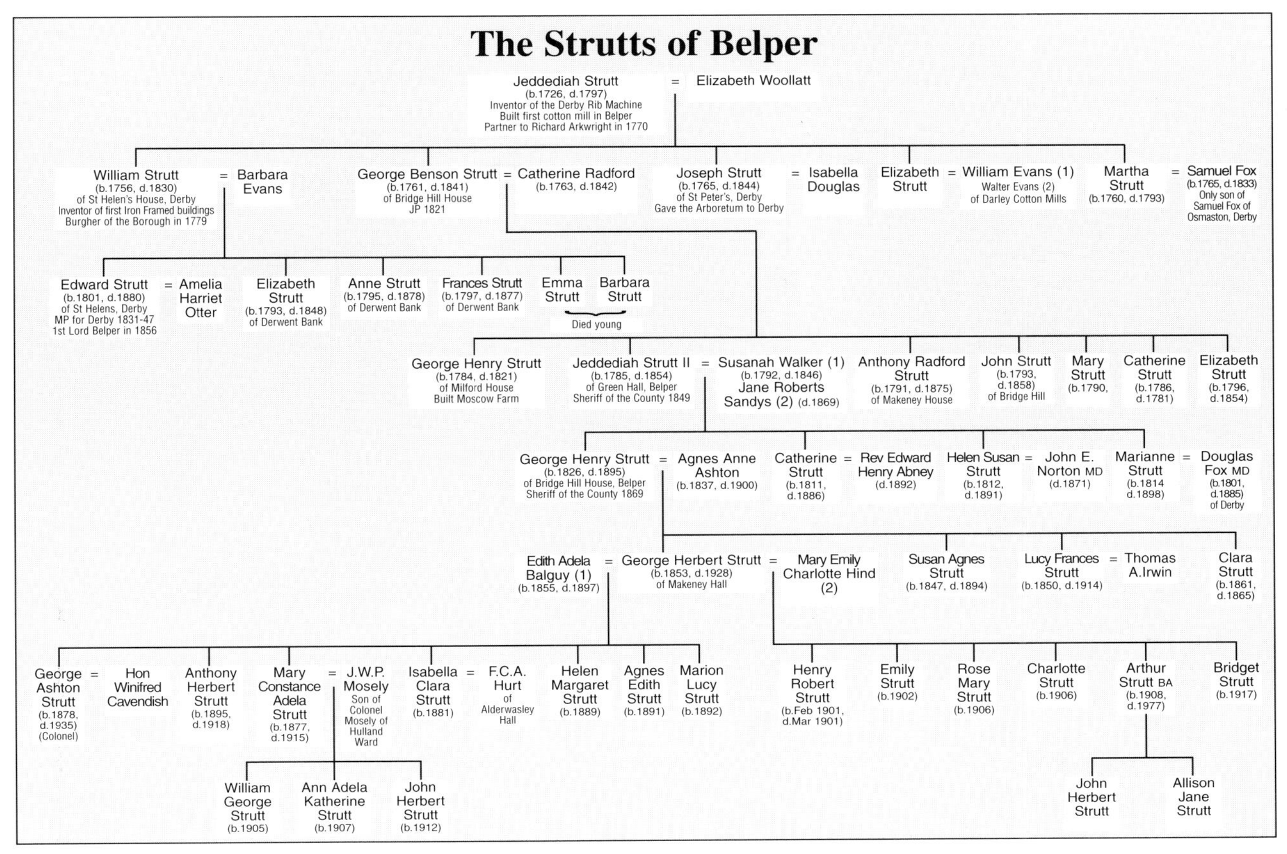

Bessalone Reservoir to Belper Town Council.

1902 Old Drill Hall erected on Clusters Road by George Herbert Strutt.

1905 George Herbert presents gift of organ to St Mark's Church, Openwoodgate. Belper Boating Association wakes and River Gardens opened by George Herbert.

1906 Arboretum and pleasure lake, grounds and tea house built in River Gardens.

1909 George Herbert Strutt School opened on Strutt plot of 'Turnip Pingle and Plantation'

1910 George Herbert Strutt donated the Gibfield Lane Swimming Baths. St John's National School rebuilt by George Herbert's donations.

1920 George Herbert gives the Memorial Gardens on King Street to the town.

1922 George Herbert bought the former Compton and Evans Bank on King Street and donated it to Belper as a War Memorial.

1922 The British Legion Club in Strutt Street built on land donated by George Herbert Strutt.

1938 Bridge Hill House demolished.

Jedediah Strutt, the son of a farmer and maltster, was born in 1726 at South Normanton. At the age of 14 he was an apprenticed journeyman to a wheelwright in Findern. He married Elizabeth Woollatt in 1755 and temporarily took up farming in the Blackwell area after an uncle died, leaving him a farm and stock. With the help of Mr Roper of Locko he began work on adapting William Lee's stocking frame to make a rib stitch and by 1758 he succeeded and patented the Derby Rib machine in joint ownership with his brother-in-law William Woollatt and the support of his partner Samuel Reed. He moved to Derby and by 1769/70 he was a well-established hosier, buying silk from East India and spinning it in his silk mill near Markeaton Brook. He had a knitted threads cottage industry and was selling the finished goods to London merchants. Now 43, he went into partnership with Richard Arkwright in 1770 and by 1771 he built the water-powered cotton spinning mill at Cromford.

In 1776, Strutt began to build his first Belper mill on the east bank of the Derwent at Belper Bridge and was in production by 1778. This was the timber-framed South Mill (rebuilt 1812). His son, William, started in the firm at the age of 14 and by the mid-1770s he played a large part in the engineering and iron-framed mill developments.

In 1780, Jedediah and Richard Arkwright dissolved their partnership. and in 1781 Strutt bought the old forge site at Makeney by Milford Bridge.

In 1786, Strutt's second mill, the North Mill, was in production and was rebuilt in 1804 after a fire. In 1788, Jedediah had the Unitarian Chapel built in Field Row and the following year 1789 his Belper mills employed 600 workers. In 1793, the mill workers houses were built in Long Row and in 1795-96 the West mill came into production.

In 1795, the gangway (linking the West and North mill areas) was built but in 1797 Jedediah died and was thought to be buried in a vault under the Unitarian Chapel. His vault was inscribed 'Founder of this Chapel. Died 1797, aged 70 years' Jedediah Strutt and his sons were the making of Belper and its industry and prosperity.

East Mill: This close-up view was sent to a Mr F.Wright, stud groom, Alderwasley, Wirksworth, in 1923 and came from 'Evelyn' at Chevin End. It clearly shows the vast expanse of this modern mill. The 1854 North Mill chimney appears above the East Mill.

It is unusual to see the title 'BBA' on photographs or postcards, but it refers to the Belper Boating Association. This view is one of the Ivanhoe Series published by J.Crowther of Rotherham in *c.*1909 and shows the River Gardens fountain with its neat, large rockery. The Jubilee Clock Tower appears along the right-angled old building associated with the South Mill. A portion of the old North Mill is visible in the distance.

Strutt's Mills: The two-horse cart has just driven through the ivy-clad arched gangway (built in 1795) across the road and is seen here alongside the rebuilt South Mill dating from 1812. This photograph, taken from the Triangle, clearly shows the iron railings and neatly kept bushes that formed a barrier from the main Ashbourne Road creating a safe walking area along side the five-storey South Mill. The high fire escape across the front of the building was a well-known feature. Note the 'penny-farthing' wheeled pram and the aproned 'child minder'. On the extreme right just out of view stood Bridge House School, a private school for ladies run by the Misses Calder (Mary Appleyard and Florence S.Calder). Locals remember that one of the ladies was rather hunch-backed and small, the other tall and wearing spectacles. At one time Mary, Florence and Jane Calder had a school at the top of Albert Street.

Clock Tower, Mill and Bridge: It is late morning and the main road from Belper to Ashbourne is completely empty in this Kingsway Series photograph of 1908. The entrance to the walkway alongside the South Mill is on the right. The bracket lamp left on the mill wall was there for many years but disappeared before World War Two. The covered wagon parked near the gangway on the right is featured in the same position over several years. Various notices have been affixed to the left-hand wall of the buildings, hiding the West, Reeling and Round Mills. Some posters might be Army Volunteer advertisements. A first-aid room for the mill workers existed in the left-hand complex at a later date.

Belper North Mill: Jedediah Strutt's second mill, originally timber-framed, built in 1786 and subsequently destroyed by fire, was rebuilt by his son, William, to his iron-framed design in 1804. The West Mill and Jubilee Clock Tower are on the right with the Round Mill, dating from 1811 just visible to the left of the Jubilee Tower. This was demolished in 1959. This extremely rare early view of the North Mill on the left was taken from the Ashbourne side of Derwent Bridge by George Julian Jackson of The Butts in late 1904. The complex array of small buildings carry various advertising plaques – 'Stockport Gas Engine; Andrew & Co Ltd', W.Jessop's filemakers of 1 Bridge Foot.

This 1905 hand-tinted view was taken from the West Mill and looks up the Derwent towards the iron railway bridge. The North Mill is on the right and the weir in the middle foreground.

Bridge Foot: After passing through the gangway across the road to Ashbourne in *c*.1910, you would have seen this fine ivy-clad building to the left prior to crossing the Derwent Bridge. On this sunny day up to a dozen Edwardian children linger long enough for George Jackson to immortalise them with his camera. The small boy on the right with dicky bow and boater appears to be holding a bunch of flowers. The culvert to the West Mill lay behind the railings on the left and the water ran under the main road to drive the water wheels to power the West Mill. The trees no longer exist.

Bridge Foot: This close up of the gangway was taken in the early 1950s. The drinking fountain on the left is inscribed 'Proposit, Teway 1858' and shows a clenched hand and arm holding a parchment (the Strutt family crest). The water appears out of the mouth of a gargoyle. The base of the Jubilee Tower is visible on the top left. By 1995, the old North Mill had various uses including a gymnasium and office suites.

Bridge Foot: This unusual view is through the mill gangway right-hand pedestrian arch looking towards the Derwent Bridge in 1936. The ivy has now been cleared away from the facia of the building on the left.

Green Walk: George J.Jackson took this photograph – this version is from a slightly fading sepia postcard – in *c*.1907-08. The message on the reverse, from 'JWS' of Farnah Green, reads: 'This is Green Walk, I go along this path every time that I visit Belper.' Green Walk was originally a private walkway leading from the magnificent Strutt's Bridge Hill House. George Benson Strutt had this elevated walkway built to allow him easy access from his lofty position down to his mills on either side of the Derwent below. The cottages through the trees on the left were once part of the cottage hospital supported and maintained by the Strutt Family. The hospice consisted of sisters' and servants' rooms, dining hall and kitchen and poor relief, either indoor or outdoor, to the aged and sick of Belper. A sister from St Laurence's Convent was in charge. In 1895 the hospital had accommodation for two indoor patients. Note the neat garden area to the left with the young bushes and conifers and newly-raked soil, ready for planting. Clients from the Cottage Hospital would sit in this pleasant area to recover from their illnesses. The walkway was built on a sturdy elevated stone foundation with what appears to be iron railings either side. The flooring looks ribbed and a hole appears to show in the foreground of this unusual walkway. The walkway still exists today but the side railings have long since gone, to be replaced by ugly concrete posts and green wire meshing. The gardens to the left are now totally overgrown, but may improve now that the present proprietor of the Talbot Inn has purchased this plot.

William Strutt, born at Blackwell near Alfreton on 20 July 1756, was the eldest of Jedediah's five children. When Jedediah died in 1797, his three sons carried on the family business under the name of W.G.& J.Strutt (William, George and Joseph) and three streets in Belper were named after them. William was the technical brains, Joseph the one with commercial expertise, whilst George was in charge of mills at Belper and Milford. William was the first person who attempted the construction of fire-proof buildings with a great deal of success, especially in his cotton mills. His first iron-framed fire-proof mill, six stories high, was built in Derby in 1793, and a four-storey mill at Milford followed by the Belper West Mill during 1793-95. The North Mill 1803-04, the Reeling Mill 1807-08 and South Mill 1811-12 followed that. William Strutt FRS was the principal director in the construction of Derby Infirmary and this was one of his greatest contributions to public life. He also helped with the design of the present St Mary's Bridge at Derby.

Wedding of Mr. J. W. P. Mosley and Miss Strutt.

APRIL 6th, 1904.

Photo by Jacolette, London.
MR. J. W. P. MOSLEY.

Photo by Lafayette.
MISS ADELA STRUTT.

Gratis Supplement to "*The Derbyshire Times*," April 9th, 1904.

Strutt wedding: This double oval for the wedding of Mr J.W.P.Mosley and Miss Adela Strutt on 6 April 1904 was given away free in the *Derbyshire Times* on 9 April 1904. Mary Constance Adela Strutt was George Herbert's first daughter of five. She died only 11 years after her marriage to the son of Colonel Mosley of Hulland Ward.

Long Row: This *c.*1915 view is taken from the top of Long Row, looking down towards Bridge Street. The Strutt family built the sturdily constructed Derbyshire gritstone three-storey housings for their mill workers. They were constructed in 1793, nearly 45 years before the construction of the North Midland railway began. The upper rooms are where the weavers toiled at their looms. 36 Long Row is on the top right (stone house) whilst numbers 40 and 41 are the brick-built houses on the top left. Some of the stone stoops where the women sat with their work still exist today. However, all of the fine looking trees on the right have disappeared, presumably to allow more light to the houses. Although not evident, there is a gap in the terracing about halfway down where houses were demolished to allow the railway to pass through. A small plaque on the abutment here reads: 'Best decorated street in Belper on the occasion of the Coronation of Queen Elizabeth II, 1953.' The Strutts saw that each house was regularly maintained by arranging for all interiors to be whitewashed each year and chimneys swept four times per year. The Strutt houses had a large square living room, a kitchen and a coal house. Each of the two upper floors was a large bedroom. Toilets were situated in the back gardens. In the late 1820s, the rent was between 2s and 2s 5½d per week. These fine terraced houses are still eagerly sought after today just as they were by Strutt's mill workers long ago.

The Clusters: These solid looking houses were built by the Strutt family in 1795. They were blocks of four houses and much larger than the mill homes of Long Row, as they were for the mill overseers. There were in fact five blocks of unusual design, with four houses in a rectangular block constructed back-to-back, two, facing on to one street, end to end, one on to another. Rents were 3s to 3s 5½d per week and 4s to 4s 8d per week according to size. The three main streets were George, William and Joseph Streets, named after Jedediah's famous sons. By 1831, Strutt owned 300 out of the 1,500 homes in Belper. This view is looking down Joseph Street from Green Lane.

Bridge Hill House: It is hard to believe that this magnificent building no longer exists, having been demolished some time after the house contents sale of 14 December 1931, organised by John D.Wood & Co. The former Bridge Hill House site is now graced by several 1930s-style houses of distinction. This view of the house was captured by George J.Jackson in 1906. The house was designed by William Strutt FRS and built in 1794 for George Benson Strutt. It was a large stone mansion, delightfully situated on a commanding eminence in park-like grounds overlooking the Derwent and Strutt's Mills complex. In its heyday the house had a vast number of servants: 17 gardeners, butler, footmen, coachman and groom, housekeeper, cook, ladies' maids, parlour maids, housemaid, laundry maids, nursery nurses, and stable boy. The grounds had greenhouses of every kind including an azelia house, melon house, geranium house, carnation house, vinery and fig house, tomato house and peach house. The large cast-iron framed Victorian conservatory was a particularly ornate later addition to the house and was filled with many tropical palms and plants together with a fountain. The Duke of Devonshire laid the first stone of St Peter's Church on 31 October 1822, after breakfasting with the Strutts at Bridge Hill House. The staunch Wesleyan Mr William Hoskins of Hazelwood possessed a good knowledge of the floral and horticultural arts and was for some time gardener at the Strutt's house and at Crich Cliff. Bridge Hill House was the seat of John Strutt, George Henry Strutt Esq JP, and eventually George Herbert Strutt Esq, DL JP VD. Three lodge houses still remain, two in Belper Lane and one on Bridge Hill. The former head gardener's home also still stands overlooking Shireoaks (a small hamlet on high ground above the Dalley). The message on the reverse side of this card is from 'W' at Bridge Hill to Mr F.Seaton of Kingairlock, Ardgour RSC, Argyllshire.

Bridge Hill House: Frederick Holbrook was commissioned to take this photograph of two of George Herbert Strutt's daughters in the mid-1920s. The young ladies on horseback are outside the main entrance with the huge Victorian conservatory hidden around the corner.

Bridge Hill House East Lodge: The stone-built East Lodge still remains in Belper Lane.

Cross Roads Farm: This charming scene shows the young Salt family at Cross Roads Farm in 1910. On horseback from left to right are Richard, William and George. The original building started life as a coaching inn and in 1846 it was recorded as the Owl Inn run by Mr William Winson. One can see the old stone Owl Inn figure in this picture. By 1857 John Winson was running the Strutt's Cross Roads model farm. William Jas Vickers had taken over at some stage prior to 1895. Some time later George Salt left Dalley Farm to live with his wife at Cross Roads (she would only marry 'if George agreed to live at Cross Roads'). He died in 1910 and Mrs George Salt took over the reigns until 1935. Cross Roads farm was a Strutt-owned farm along with Dalley, Wyver, and Moscow Farms, and were used in order to offer their workers fresh produce at reasonable rates. In 1894, Charles Willot recorded that Cross Roads Farm had been successively held by Winsons, Strettons, Halls and Vickers.

This magnificent stone built house pictured here by Burkinshaw in 1907 was attached to the old Dalley Farm *c.*1897. The house is much the same today with all the windows and doors replaced in modern form but tastefully in keeping similar to the original designs. The small pathway has been replace by a much wider drive. The old lean-to greenhouse on the left has been replaced by a small modern unit. The garden seat still exists, although in a different part of the garden, having received recent renovation. The pot gable finials still exist but are leaning somewhat. Mr John Fletcher is the owner of this fine property. The owner prior to 1913 was George Allsop. A large 'monkey tree' stood on the left-hand side but has since been removed.

This Burkinshaw photograph of 1907 clearly shows where the old original Dalley Farm house, built *c.*1764, joins the new house of 1897. To the right is one wall of a narrow walled channel leading to the original farmhouse door. A little of the iron supports and fencing can still be found. Some of Dalley's outbuildings contain important structural features. One open-fronted barn is iron-framed with support pillars reminiscent of William Strutt's work dated 1857, and an adjacent building has a mysterious iron support bracket dated 1836. Dalley was a Strutt's 'home farm', producing food for the Strutt family rather than their workers. At John Fletcher's (the current owner) recent farm sale an important early hay and straw chopping machine, made by William Holdens & Sons of Belper, was unearthed and sold to the Belper Heritage and Visitors' Centre for preservation.

The Dalley was a small hamlet in the township of Belper and consisted of about ten homes situated on the main road about a quarter of a mile from Belper Lane End. From here on the high ground, good views of Crich may be had. In 1894, Charles Willot wrote of Dalley Farm, pictured here: 'Thought at first to originally belong to a Mr Launder then Benjamin Gillot. Squire Norton purchased it and many years later it was put up for sale by auction at Mr John Frost's house (who was a farmer on Belper Lane). Mr John Strutt outbid Mr Frost and gave £84 an acre. Strutt rebuilt Dalley Farm. In the early nineteenth century a great amount of stocking work was carried on here by the Morell family. The old kitchen and dairy were used as a shop. After Gillot came three generations of Coopers. The present tenant is Mr Salt.'

John Strutt also acquired the Dalley Pit coalfields, possibly five or six in number worked by whimsey or gin-race! Thus Dalley Farm had had a colourful existence by 1894.

George Cooper was recorded in 1846, Samuel Cooper by 1857 and Jarman Cooper by 1888. George Salt was listed in 1895 with George Allsop by 1912. In 1913, William Salt farmed here until the present Fletcher family. The magnificent stone paved yard and outbuildings remain largely intact. The huge circular stone trough has been resited and the dog kennel, built into the left-hand wall, removed. A clock face was installed in the centre apex sometime c.1930, together with a weather vane on the apex. The bracket lamp just above the stone staircase to the left is lost but the large iron-framed window with small centre opening remains. Some of the yard has been concreted over since this 1907 Burkinshaw photograph was taken. The message on the reverse side, sent to a Mrs Holt, Parkhill, Hasland, reads: 'I stayed at Dally last night. Shall be home perhaps Monday.'

Quarry Bank: This fine stone building is now part of St Elizabeth's Catholic School and is situated off Matlock Road just past the railway bridge as you leave Belper going north, and is hidden behind trees. Quarry Bank House was the former residence of John Hunter JP OBE MICE FRMS. Prior to the turn-of-the-century he was a trusted agent of W.G. & J.Strutt (Jedediah's three sons) living at Northfield Villa on Matlock Road. Shortly after 1900 he made Quarry Bank his home where he stayed until his death in 1937. He was chairman of Belper UDC in 1928 (after George Herbert Strutt) having being the vice-chairman for many years, as well as a local JP. The Belper Humane Society was established in 1824 for providing clean bed linen for the poor of the town, together with a nursing association and supported by voluntary subscription. John Hunter was secretary to this society from *c.*1910 to the 1930s. He was born the same year as George Herbert Strutt and little was he to know at the time that he would be governor of the Herbert Strutt School from its inception in 1909 through to 1937; he was also private secretary to G.H.Strutt for many years. He was recorded as vice-president to Herbert Strutt of the Belper Natural History and Philosophical Society, which was established in 1878. He was chairman of the management committee of the Belper Schools in 1915. He died on 12 March 1937 at the age of 83. Following the Strutt tradition he bequeathed to the school governors £100 consolidated 2½ per cent stock 'to be applied by them at their discretion in providing a prize to be called the John Hunter Memorial Prize'. The message on the reverse side is from 'Polly' to Miss Jennison of Bridge Street. Thomas Jennison had a fancy draper's shop in Bridge Street and was a previous High Bailiff to the County Court. The card records: 'Thought you would like this view of Quarry Bank. Hasn't it been cold? Have you been to see the soldiers yet?' The photograph was by William Samuel Bowler and was posted on 8 June 1905, and shows Mr and Mrs Hunter on the drive.

View from Bridge Hill: This *c.*1911 view taken from Bridge Hill shows the stone arched Derwent Bridge and River Gardens beyond. More importantly it shows the old terraced and other stone houses along Cemetery Lane and Swinney Lane near Fieldhead. The distant horizon is quite clear, proving that the Crich Lane dwellings are yet to be built. For reasons unknown the area between Cemetery Lane and Swinney Lane was always called Penny Corn. The North Mill complex is hidden behind the right-hand trees.

View from Bridge Hill: The old Cottage Hospital cottages are visible in the centre. Behind the trees is Belper Cemetery mortuary chapel. What a difference 50 years can make: the horizon and area around Crich Lane and Cemetery and Swinney Lanes now contains many new houses. The wooded area top left is that of Swinney Wood.

The Bridge: The ancient bridge over the River Derwent on which was affixed the supposed arms of John of Gaunt – by whom it was allegedly built – was destroyed by a great flood in 1795 and succeeded by a handsome stone bridge of three arches. This early and important stone was removed and placed in the gable of Benjamin Marshall's house in Belper Lane. The new bridge was constructed between 1796 and 1798 by Isaac and Benjamin Marshall at a total cost of £2,180. The Horseshoe Weir, built in 1797, lies behind in this *c.*1909 photograph by G.J.Jackson.

The Bridge and Weir: This *c.*1912-13 Kingsway Series photograph is looking north up river towards Ambergate and the intricate weir mechanisms were to the left on top of the neatly constructed weir arches. The Horseshoe Weir is to the right with the iron railway bridge visible in the distance. This photographic postcard was sent by Isabel to the Revd H.E.Field of St Anne's Vicarage, Ambergate.

Bridge Foot: Harold Burkinshaw took this shadowy scene of Bridge Foot on a quiet day *c.*1908. The old cast-iron French style urinal stood adjacent to the lamp standard at the intersection of Bridge Hill and Belper Lane. This was a unique scene for many years and is remembered by many of the older Belper inhabitants. The row of cottages ascending up the hill of the old coach road running between Wirksworth and Derby are all ivy-clad in this view. At one time a toll gate existed at Bridge Foot to control the steep route out of Belper.

Bridge Foot: The Talbot Inn (now called the Talbot Hotel) stands on the left of this Kingsway Series photograph at the bottom of Bridge Hill and is Belper's oldest public house. The stone building is L-shaped and in this *c*.1914-15 view the inn sign is hung from the right-hand section whereas today it is on the left. The sign now shows a dog similar to a retriever breed but is in fact a 'Talbot', an extinct hunting dog. The sign over the door denotes that Thomas Allsop was in charge. The stone lintel over the door of the Talbot is inscribed 'T.C.1867'. However, this must be a later addition as the original stone is inserted in the wall to the right of the door forming a kissing stone inscribed: '1660 G.F.Frost'. The right-hand arched doorway is now hidden by a small tasteful porch. The right-hand lower window, bricked up in this view, is now restored. The ancient sycamore and stone seats in front of the Talbot are mentioned in Charles Willott's book *Belper and its People* (1894). To the right of the Talbot, the demolition of a fine stone wall and small outbuilding belonging to the tall three-storey house is well under way. The gap between the inn and the house was used for turning the horses around. Alas, today the gap is no more; Louise Carol's modern beauty salon has been built there and looks incongruous between the ancient inn and house. The lower windows of the Talbot have been changed from small paned to large sash types and the shutters have been removed. The remnants of the old cast-iron Vaspasienne French-style toilet adjacent to the centre lamp standard are clearly visible. The gas lamp on the left lit the area leading to a gents' toilet which replaced the former cast-iron toilet (all has now gone). The last cottage up Belper Lane has also had its small wood and glass porch removed.

Bridge Foot: This photograph was issued by R.Sneath of Sheffield and shows the Bridge Foot and Belper Lane leading to the pleasant hamlet of Belper Lane End situated approximately one mile from Belper. The horse and cart are level with the opening of Wyver Lane: note the fine curved wall and shaped bush and hedging in front of the neat three-storey house standing close to the Talbot Inn. This postcard publication, originally sepia, was sent by 'Alice' from 4 Nether Lawn, Belper Lane. The former Strutts Cottage Hospital stands on the right.

Belper Lane: Very little has changed in this early 1944 photograph by Valentine & Sons. The lamp standard at the intersection now carries signposts for Ashbourne and Derby. The fine old tree on the right near the cottage hospital has been cut down. However, the land on the left adjoining Green Walk has been cleared and new conifers are noticeable. The former Strutt's Cottage Hospital – now three cottages – is visible on the right. Flags are hanging outside the Talbot Inn and also from one of the former hospital cottages.

Belper Lane: The three small children cower from the photographer in the vicinity of Bridge Foot. This early 1930s view looks up Belper Lane towards the Scotches with Wyver Lane off to the right. The railings in the near corner of Wyver Lane have been there for some considerable time. It is not clear why the walling wasn't continued around.

Wyver Lane (Wild Boar Lane): This photographic postcard by Lilywhite Ltd was posted by 'M.L.' in 1944 and the message reads: 'I expect your mother will tell you. She's had many a picnic down this lovely lane and gathered bluebells too.' The first three cottages on the left are numbers 3, 5 and 7 and still look good today. The two-gabled building, built in 1899, contains numbers 9, 11 and 13; Number 13, the right-hand gable, has an old rusting sign 'Fireman No.9' above it. Weir View Cottage and York Cottage are in this lane. A firing range for the Territorials existed towards the end of this lane. Today Wyver Pool is the Derbyshire Wildlife Trust's nature reserve.

Wyver Lane from the River Gardens, *c.*1950, showing the modern building erected between the Talbot Inn and the adjacent three-storey house.

Wyver Lane from the Rockery in 1907-08. The photograph was by Burkinshaw, published by Stewart Gibson, the stationers, in Bridge Street.

Another Burkinshaw photograph, showing Belper Pool and swans with Wyver Lane visible through the trees *c.*1920..

Belper River Gardens

In 1904, George Herbert Strutt donated the site and the initial development of the boating station and landing stage took place, affording three miles of boating. The grand opening by G.H.Strutt took place in 1905 and the occasion was celebrated with a 'grand water carnival' and a competition for decorated floats. Several eminent local businessmen entered their creations: Harold Burkinshaw (photographer) entered a 20ft-long swan, whilst James Pym (wine and spirits merchant) supplied a floating pagoda with 200 fairy lamps. During 1906 the site was further developed to provide pleasure grounds and an arboretum. A bandstand, fountain, grottoes and promenades were also installed to the great delight of the 8,000 people who turned up on Easter Monday 1906. Many celebrations were held here over the ensuing years. For nearly 90 years now the River Gardens with its boating, concerts and strolls along Serpentine Walk have been a source of pleasure for generations of local people. At some stage a 10d fee was charged to enter these gardens.

River Gardens: This originally coloured publication was an official issue by the Midland Railway and is titled 'Pleasure Gardens Belper, Derbyshire'. (The station is now on the Midland Main Line between London and the north.) The Midland Railway Company's 'Wyvern' crest is on the reverse side of the card with the following statement: 'The Best Route for Comfortable Travel and Picturesque Scenery.' The illustration is taken from an original painting and shows local Belper people enjoying a day out on the river.

River Gardens: This early sepia view of the fountain and bandstand formed part of a Stereoscopic card produced by J.Siddons of Saltley, Birmingham. The band are in position and several well-dressed locals are in the vicinity to hear them playing.

River Gardens: The magnificent thatched tea house with well-dressed serving ladies was recorded through the lens of George Jackson in this early 1906 photograph. Only a year after construction, the deep heather thatch was replaced by tiles due to the ingress of water. The three gentlemen on the right of the picture take time out in the sun awaiting the next concert at 3pm. The thatched tea house was advertised as the 'Swiss tea house'. The poster under the verandah advertises 'The Grand Venetian Water Fete for Belper Wakes'. Allegedly, one could get a cup of tea here for a penny until many years after World War Two.

River Gardens: William Samuel Bowler, chemist and photographer of Bridge Street, took this view *c.*1908. Several people are strolling along the water's edge. Note the fine wooden lattice-work curved fencing in front of the bandstand; this has now disappeared. The original thatched tea house is now tiled. The wooden bandstand and tea house are still 99 per cent original today with only minor additions. Bowler's photographs are usually identified by his use of titles in purple ink or a purple circular address to the rear.

The bandstand: The band are playing beneath the copper canopy of the bandstand in the River Gardens whilst ten local ladies listen to their music. One assumes that the umbrellas must be open to protect them from the sun rather than rain. There are literally hundreds of chairs stacked around the bandstand, ready for one of the band's well-attended weekend concerts. Note the many hanging baskets suspended around the bandstand canopy.

The bandstand and fountain: The fountain is in full flow on this sunny day in 1908 at Belper's Boating Association Gardens. A canvas screen is in place to shield the band from the sun. The copper canopy was a real work of art, and is in fine order today, although the small embellishments at each corner are now lost.

The bandstand is covered in fairy lights and bunting can be seen around the tea house in this 1908 Valentines publication. In its heyday the River Gardens boasted of up to 15,000 lights being displayed. The gentlemen on the seat worked here tending the various needs within the River Gardens complex.

Landing stage: The bearded boatman (believed to be John McArthur) is standing on a floating platform organising the boats with his hooked pole. Harold Burkinshaw has recorded the fine wooden decking of the original landing stage in this 1906 scene. Alas, the decking has now been replaced by a functional concrete surface. 'BBA' is clearly printed on the lifebelt housed at the end of the landing stage. The five boats are but a year old. Note the stout rope tied to the tree on the left.

River Gardens: The Boating Association superintendent, together with a man in bowler hat, stand along side the boats *c.*1908 Two-seater and four-seater boats are in view along with the small 'Mayfly' and large 'Derwent'. Note the fine wooden lattice-work circular seating around some of the trees. Some of the existing boats today bear a small metal plaque with 'Elton Boats, Wyver Lane, Belper, Derbyshire' inscribed.

Boating stage: The boatman sporting his BBA shirt stands with his young assistant for this 1915 Kingsway photograph. The small house on the left, where people paid to hire the boats, is still there today and contains the original desk. The unusual feature of this photograph is the cat-like creature floating in the water to the far right. Presumably this must have been a float from one of the various fetes held here. Today's charges of £3.20 per hour and £1.95 per half-hour for one or two people to hire the boats appear to be quite reasonable.

Belper Pool and landing stage: The tea house hidden by the trees is still thatched in this 1906 Burkinshaw photograph. The message on the reverse reads: 'This is a view of our river. It is a lovely spot. I would be pleased if you would join us next Saturday for a picnic and trip on the river.' Small sailing ships were occasionally seen in the Belper Pool, but may have been privately owned. The many latticed seats around the trees are evident in this view.

Belper Carnival: This Loch Ness Monster look-alike was probably destined to form a float for one of the water carnivals held in the River Gardens *c.*1906-07 during Belper Wakes Week. The message on the reverse side reads: 'Nelli come kiss your baby; Kiss him good and fine; press bofe dose ruby lips to mine; sey ain't you glad you've found me?' Harold Burkinshaw recorded this close up view of the monster, The reference to 'Inspector Wappadoodle of the Boarding Dept' was no doubt a 'dig' at a member of the BBA.

This scene is possibly one of the early Belper Wakes with hundreds of people gathered on the landing stage. This large boat (probably named 'Derwent', see earlier photograph) has an unbelievable 40 people on board together with a large wind-up gramophone player. The young man with boater appears to be leading from his song sheet on this happy occasion on Belper Pool *c.*1906-07.

Boating Stage: Three young Belper locals (one wearing a black armband) wait patiently on the wooden staging whilst their boat is prepared. The boatman's assistant, in white sleeves and cap, is making the necessary booking on his wooden lectern affixed to the end of the floating boating stage.

POST CARD

TO BE USED FOR WRITTEN OR PRINTED MATTER | ONLY THE ADDRESS TO BE WRITTEN HERE.

INLAND POSTAGE ½d.
FOREIGN POSTAGE 1d.

Belper River Gardens.

Don't fail to come and hear the Famous Band of

H. M. 2nd Seaforth Highlanders

Boat Racing Dancing & Illuminations.

WAKES WEDNESDAY, JULY 9th, 1913.

R. B. MUIR, Hon. Sec.

This is the fine figure of T.B.F.Wiltshire, the bandmaster of the 2nd Seaforth Highlanders, one of many first-class bands to appear at the Belper River Gardens concerts. The Grenadiers, Coldstream and Scots Guards all played here as well as the local Belper Prize Band during the many summer concerts.

The 2nd Seaforth Highlanders were playing on Wakes Wednesday, 9 July 1913.

River Gardens: At the boathouse end of the River Gardens an extensive plot of ground with a stage for outdoor performances existed. Harold Burkinshaw has recorded this pre-1920s scene where many Belper folk have turned out to watch the stage performances. In this scene it appears to be a policeman and Scottish soldier on stage with the piano player on the right. The people in the foreground are standing on an iron lattice-work bridge with railing down the centre which crossed the 'Cut' sluice. The Bridge itself is still in situ today but decay is evident and the centre railings have gone, forcing the area to be closed off.

Wakes celebrations: Many hundreds of Belper and area locals appear in this view of the Wakes Concert recorded by Fred Holbrook *c.*1913. The reverend is on the left with the band in the foreground, being a mix of military and civilians. Trumpets, trombones and three violin players are there, together with a small 'squeeze box' (played by the gentlemen on the left with the trilby hat). One poor boy, situated three back from the right-hand trombone player, appears to have suffered a broken jaw or severe toothache judging by the large white bandage wrapped around his chin and head.

The Riverside Pavilion: Over 20 soldiers from various regiments and including two sailors are in the large crowd gathered outside the pavilion in the River Gardens *c.*1918. In its early days the pavilion was used as a canteen to the mill. Mr Holbrook was again the photographer who recorded the scene which probably formed part of the Wakes celebrations or victory celebrations. The pavilion was situated at the East Mill end of the River Gardens and was reached by the lattice work bridge over the 'Cut' sluice seen in the previous view. Note the ornate cast-iron construction to the right surmounted by a large lamp. Many older Belper folk can remember going to the pavilion to see pierrots and to many concerts, where the Billy Joyce Band played. The famous Marty Wilde performed here in the late 1950s. The dance floor was apparently very beautiful, and it was one of Belper's first places to stay open until 1am.

The Pavilion: The gaslit verandah of the Riverside pavilion is the scene of a grand tea, captured here by Harold Burkinshaw in *c.*1915. The ladies have just finished their main course as the maid brings out the pudding. Much tea is being drunk, the teapot being topped up from the large copper urn on the end of the table. There is plenty of bread and butter, scones and jam for the 30 or so ladies. The men appear to be seated just out of view at the top left where the bar was situated. The actual event is unknown.

Places of Worship

Belper has four main churches, three mission churches and several free churches representing the Wesleyans, Methodists, Baptists and Unitarians.

St John's: The old chapel of St John the Baptist situated on the Butts was probably founded *c.*1250 by Edmund Crouchback, second son of Henry III. The remains of 53 Belper victims of the 1609 plague are situated here. The building is in the Early English lancet style consisting of chancel and nave under a single roof, south porch (1634) and a bell cote (1699) on the western gable, containing one bell, inscribed: 'God save his church 1699'. A wooden gallery was added *c.*1806 at the west end of the nave and a vestry about the same time. The gallery was demolished in the 1870s. The chapel was partly restored in 1866 by the Revd Robert Hey MA, vicar of Belper 1845-85. Florence Nightingale sent £2 towards the 1866 restoration. The church was again restored in 1922 under the advice and care of the Society for the Preservation of Ancient Buildings. Colonel Hunter OBE supervised the work which was carried out by local builder J.Haynes. At this time an old nailers' iron cross was found in the churchyard and was originally set on top of the bell cote as seen in this *c.*1916 view by Valentine. The chancel screen and encaustic tiles were removed, the floor repaired with stone slabs and the interior reseated with oak. This restoration, together with a new lych gate erected in the memory of Mr Isaac Hanson (managing director of George Brettle & Co), cost approximately £1,400. The increase in Belper's population created by the mills eventually made St John's inadequate, and in 1822-24, St Peter's Church was built. The church was used for special services and meetings up to the mid-1980s, later becoming redundant, but happily was refurbished and opened as the present-day Heritage Centre and Belper Town Council Chamber now under the diligent care of Jackie Woodward.

St Peter's Church was built in 1822 at a cost of £11,921, most of which came from a government grant. The Duke of Devonshire laid the foundation stone on 31 October 1822 and the church was dedicated in 1824. It is a handsome stone edifice in the Gothic Decorated style. The stone was obtained from Hunger Hill Quarry, half a mile away. It consisted of nave and a western tower 100ft high with pinnacles containing a clock and six bells dating from 1861. The nave was embattled with pinnacles adorning the four corners, although all the pinnacles were removed during World War Two. The chancel is a deep recess, abutting at the east end. The ground stage of the tower forms a porch.

St Peter's Church (interior): The east window of five lights, tracery headed filled with stained glass and to the north of it, was a memorial tablet to Jedediah Strutt II Esq and to the south, there is one to his wife Susannah Strutt. A gallery runs around three sides and underneath it on the east wall of the nave is placed a chaste marble monument to George Brettle who died in 1835. The organ was placed in the west gallery and dated from 1853, being one of the earliest large organs in the country and was fully restored in 1979. The church was furnished with seats of pitchpine and the octagonal stone font was placed in the west gallery underneath the organ.

Christ Church, Bridge Hill, was an Ecclesiastical parish formed on 3 September 1845 out of Duffield parish, the church being a substantial stone edifice, was built by public subscription in 1849 in Bridge Street near the Triangle. It is oblong, strongly buttressed, with a bell turret at the west end containing three bells, and a porch at the south-west. It is of the Early English style consisting of chancel nave and vestry (added in 1904), and cost £3,000. The church was restored in 1876-77 at a cost £2,000. The chancel was separated from the nave by an iron screen on a basement of stone. The floor rose one step above that of the nave and was laid out with encaustic tiles of the fourteenth century. The chancel was furnished with open vale pews and the organ stands at either corner being installed in 1850 and replaced some 20 years later. The east window, one of three lights, was pointed and filled with ornamental glass. The nave was furnished with pews of pitchpine and lighted by five pointed, one-light windows. The font, made of Caen stone, circular in shape and elaborately sculptured, stood at the west end. The Strutt family made the following gifts to Christ Church: Public palls, bier, shrouds, windows, altar and candlesticks. The Strutt family, with their seat in Bridge Hill, used to worship here and the Vicarage on the left of this 1906 Burkinshaw photograph was the gift of George Herbert Strutt Esq JP and was held at this time by the Revd Edward Augustus Hillyard BA. The Vicarage was a substantial stone residence and has a small plaque beneath the raised bay window inscribed 'Fear God'. George Herbert Strutt died at the age of 75 and his funeral was held at Christ Church.

Belper's Congregational Church (Chapel) is situated in Green Lane (formerly Market Street Lane) and was erected in 1872 complete with schoolroom, replacing an older chapel erected in 1790. It is built of stone and originally cost £5,000 and is of the Early English style, seating up to 600 persons. The graceful tower and spire rise to a height of 120ft. The east window contained three lights, the tracery work being filled with ornamental glass. The chancel arch is lofty and pointed, on either side of which is a window of one light, in the east wall of the nave. The side walls each contain six large two-light, pointed, tracery headed windows. The west window is a very large, one of four lights. The interior was refurbished in 1886. The chancel contained a sweet-toned organ with the inscription 'Presented to the Congregational Church by Ebenezer Smedley Esq, 26 May 1886'. Ebenezer Arthur Smedley lived at Park Villa, New Road. In this *c.*1913 view by Kingsway, the Revd Charles A.Porteous would have led the proceedings. The church with its Gothic turret now lies redundant and is believed to have been sold. The small group of Congregationalists now meet in a small modern building at the rear.

Christ Church, Belper.

—★—

DEAR FRIEND,

This is to wish you a very happy Easter and a glorious Communion.

Will you (1) try to come to Church once every day in Holy Week ?

(2) try to attend the Communion Preparation at 8.30 on Thursday ?

(3) join in our Procession of Witness on Good Friday evening ?

(4) discourage all attempts of others to make Good Friday a holiday ?

Confessions may be heard every day in Holy Week and the times will be on the Church Notice Board. If you have given up this Sacrament, God is calling you back to it. Think it out on your knees.

Yours affectionately

H. S. G. WALKER,

Parish Priest.

925. Printed by the Faith Press, Ltd., Leighton Buzzard, England.

Christ Church: This late 1920s religious card with a coloured picture of Christ on the front, with the message 'Death is Swallowed Up in Victory', was handed out just prior to Easter. Since 1927 the Vicarage living was held by the Revd Herbert Storrs Gerald Walker BA of Hatfield Hall, Durham. Note item 4 on the card – 'Discourage all attempts of others to make Good Friday a holiday?'

St Laurence's Convent: The Anglican convent of the Sisters of St Laurence, situated in Field Lane, near the Railway Station, is a fine building of stone three stories high, erected in 1882/85 at a cost of £12,000. The sisters were engaged in parochial visiting and nursing. The rule of the sisters was based on that of East Grinstead. It was erected on land purchased from the Strutt family. The foundress and first mother superior was Ellen Lee, who died in 1901. Edward E.Bowler took this photograph in the early 1920s and shows the mother superior sitting on the left with her attendant, while in the right a bowler-hatted gentleman tends the flower beds. Nearly every window appears to have a window box full of flowers. The facia was covered over in ivy at the end of the Victorian period.

St Laurence's Convent: The chapel was prettily arranged, and contained several stained glass windows in the north and south walls and an organ at the west end. The message to the reverse recalls: 'Dear Mary, I promised you a picture of our lovely chapel last year and could not get one, however this is a recent one, Love from Nellie.' The card was again by Edward Bowler and posted on 29 May 1908.

Belper cyclists: This Burkinshaw *c.*1912 photograph shows an unknown Belper reverend and his family, each with their fine bicycles of various types.

Convent of St Laurence: The following two illustrations are relatively modern, being published during the mid to late-1960s. One of the messages on the reverse reads: 'Dear Pop, arrived here yesterday at 4.45. The Revd Mother and Sisters send their best wishes to you. I think its raining outside but I'm not sure as its still dark. I arrived just in time for two huge helpings of farm house soup. Sister Joyce has just given me a knock, Mass at 7.30am. Oh Well!!!'

This group of seven church-going young ladies with their vicar and possibly his wife came from the collection of Miss Emma White of 5 Joseph Street, Belper who is on the right of the back row. It is possibly a confirmation class associated with St Peter's Church. The vicar is perhaps Revd Stuart Harrington Clarke and the date *c*.1912.

Salvation Army: The hard working and well-respected Salvation Army representatives of Belper were photographed here by Frederick Holbrook *c*.1912. The Salvation Army barracks were first situated in King Street, in what was formerly the Gaiety Music Hall near the Railway Hotel. The Salvation Army citadel is now situated on the Market Place on the site of the former notorious Angel Inn. Gladys Blount of St John's Road vividly recalls the happy times enjoying a pea supper in the Salvation Army's wooden hut at the side of the Market Place quarters.

Methodists

The early Methodists had a circuit in Belper district being part of the 'Derbyshire Round'. Thomas Slater, a farmer of Shottle, was undoubtedly the first Methodist in the neighbourhood and in 1767 he opened his own house, known as the Chapel Farm, Shottle, for divine worship. The probable date for the introduction of Methodism into Belper was 1770 and Thomas Slater was an active agent in originating the Methodist Society in Belper. It was at the same time as the advent of the Strutts and the building of the first of their mills, rapidly converting a struggling hamlet into the second largest town in the county.

The Market Place being the chief resort, services were regularly held there, and also in a cottage in Chapel Street, and a butcher's shop in Wellington Court. At the time there was no place of worship in the town except the Old Chapel of Ease on the Butts (St John's) and a small room in Green Lane, which was once the Unitarian School room and which had been used by a variety of Nonconformists since 1721.

In 1839 the centenary of the commencement of Methodism was celebrated and the Belper Circuit contributed £543 11s 5d to a central fund which raised £216,000. Preaching places existed at Pottery, Buckland Hollow, Toad Moor, Sandy Ford, Dally Street and Belper Bridge.

The United Methodist Church (Salem) was erected in Green Lane at the junction of Field Lane in 1856. Francis White in his 1857 *Gazetteer and Directory* refers to this church as the Wesleyan Reform Church in Market Street Lane 'now in the course of erection at a cost of about £1,000 with seating for about 700 persons'. *Bulmer's Directory* of 1895 refers to it as the United Methodist Free Church or Salem Chapel, being a large rectangular brick building. The front of this chapel was in two tiers, the upper one containing three semi-circular windows, and the lower tier two square ones. A gallery ran around three sides, and the interior was furnished with seats of pitchpine, whilst a rostrum of timber stood at the west end. Underneath the chapel there was a Sunday School and class rooms. The chapel was demolished *c.*1966 along with the Methodist's Field Head Chapel and the site now forms part of the St Laurence Convent garden. This view was published by Randolph C.Neild of Ripley *c.*1914. The Revd Thomas Skillings was here prior to 1895, with the Revd John Hammond, the minister from Albion Villas, following on. By 1912 the Revd James W.Neild had taken over and by 1928 the Revd William Reuben Smith was *in situ*.

REV. W. R. SMITH.
GLENHOLMS,
21, ALBERT STREET,
BELPER, NR. DERBY.

July 14 31

Dear Ron

You hide your light under a bushel, or is it that I have been pacing about the County of late, & have not heard the things that have come to pass in Belper in these days? I had not heard of your great achievement until the local press blazoned it from the house tops.

POST CARD.

THE ADDRESS TO BE WRITTEN ON THIS SIDE.

Very Hearty Congratulations. You have done magnificently, bringing honour to Belper, & all its people, as well as to the family of Salem. It is a triumphal beginning to a coveted career. All success to you in the future stages

with Best of Wishes

W R Smith

Salem Chapel: This postcard was sent by the Salem Chapel minister William Reuben Smith in 1931 from his home at Glenholm, 21 Albert Street, and reads: 'Dear Ron, You hide your light under a bushel, or is it I have been pacing about the County of late. I have not heard the things that have come to pass in Belper in these days. I had not heard of your great achievement until the local press blazoned it from the house tops. Very hearty congratulations. You have done magnificently, bringing honour to Belper and all its people, as well as to the family of Salem. It is a triumphal beginning to a coveted career. All success to you in the future. With Best Wishes, W.R.Smith.'

Salem Chapel: This fine early photograph was specially commissioned from gold medal photographer Frederick J.Boyes of 22/24 Osmaston Road, Derby, and came from the Stevenson family (dyers). This year, 1900, was the Salem Sunday School anniversary and two sermons were to be held on 27 May 1900. A public tea and meeting for the spring session was also to be held on 16 May 1900. There are only ten ladies out of this fine gathering of approximately 60 Methodist worshippers. Both 60-year-old James Henry Stevenson and 29-year-old James Francis Stevenson, his third, son, are believed to be in this strong Methodist gathering. These two played a large part in the local Methodist movement and held many official positions in the area.

The 1887 Jubilee: This was another privately commissioned photograph from the Stevenson family. Out of the 50 men, including two boys, only three are without beard or moustache. The flags are out for this gathering in honour of Queen Victoria's Jubilee Year of 1887. This is almost certainly a Methodist gathering, possibly at the Salem Chapel in Green Lane.

Old Chapel House: Situated on Chapel Street, this is still in existence. It was one of the Methodist movement's first places of worship and now forms part of the Belper Cottage Project. This is an ecumenical project jointly managed and run by the churches of Belper with assistance from community and statutory body representatives. It exists to serve the needs of Belper people with personal problems.

Central Methodist Church: The original chapel was built in 1782 on Chapel Street, the site being given by Thomas Slater, the Shottle farmer and Methodist. An old memorandum book of his records the principal sums of cash for the building works were paid to Obediah Wigley (joiner), Abram Harrison (for nails), Thomas Pedley (for bricks and lime), the total being £135 18s 11d. Among the subscriptions paid were Thomas Gillot (£3 3s), potter William Bourne (£15), and framework knitter Joseph Statham (£3 3s). Tradition states that John Wesley preached here on behalf of the chapel before it was finished. However, his only recorded visit was in 1786. The old chapel remained in use for 25 years and in 1805 it was found necessary to secure adjoining land and build a larger chapel. This illustration shows this larger chapel which opened on 28 June 1807, at a cost of £3,000. With but few alterations it remained much the same for many years. It was built to seat 1,400 and was the wonder of the country for many miles around. It was a handsome stone building and in 1841 a large school room was erected behind the chapel.

Central Methodist Church (interior): In 1844, an organ was placed behind the pulpit in the gallery and two burial grounds attached with a chapel house for the minister at a total cost of £5,500. It had a fine gallery running round in the shape of a horseshoe. In 1873 it was modernised, the whole of the building being pewed, a new organ erected and a porch built at a total outlay of £850.

Pottery Wesleyan Chapel was built in 1816 and furnished with pitchpine pews, and an organ at the east end. A gallery ran all round and accommodated 250 worshippers. The chapel was established mainly through the efforts of the Bourne family who first established their potteries here. The schoolroom was built in 1870. The chapel porch was the gift of the late Mr Reuben Spencer, a prominent Manchester citizen who had a successful career at the Pottery School. The chapel is now in a state of decay and closed in 1990.

Lane End Chapel: The chapel was built in 1849 at a cost of £136 and Joseph Riley was the leader for 40 years. The Sunday School was opened in 1856. The chapel was well lighted and furnished, affording accommodation for 130 worshippers. The 1903 chronicles records: 'Owing to a number of removals the work here suddenly collapsed and the place is unfortunately closed. At the moment of writing (1903) there is a probability of the Chapel being re-opened. There is room for Methodism in this isolated hamlet and workers are volunteering their services.'

The Parks: This late Victorian photograph gives a clear view of Coppice Brook. A young boy is standing on the ancient footbridge across the brook, whilst another has come down the steep footpath from Ladywell. The area looks tidy and well managed. The area used to be part of a medieval Deer Park and dense woodland formerly known as Lady Park. The Lady Well area had a never-failing spring until it was demolished by Belper Waterworks Co in 1886 to utilise the water, the area becoming a reservoir. The area was a favourite spot for courting couples and lovers. New Breck is a beautiful area near here.

Belper from the Parks: This Valentine's publication shows The Fleet, Belper, in the mid-1920s. The houses from Fleet Crescent (left) down to Manor Road are all relatively new council properties and all are in existence today. However, all buildings from Manor Road to Days Lane are lost with Harry Flanders & Co's hosiery buildings replacing most of them. Queen Street leads off from here up to New Road. The new Fleet Park flats have been built on the right, replacing the stone buildings on the edge of the Park. The Jubilee Tower and East Mill are visible to the top right and the Unity Mill chimney in the centre and Brettle's factory on the left. Fleet Road eventually leads to the area of Cow Hill, out of view on the left.

Nottingham and Spencer Roads: this rare *c.*1908 view by an unknown photographer shows Nottingham Road (foreground) and Spencer Road (background) running parallel with each other as they merge on the right in the area known as The Gutter. The volume of former Common Land between the two roads is clearly evident. Where the High Street ends and Spencer Road commences, used to be called Top Common. This view taken from the land at the rear of Mill Lane shows Park Mount and Fred Blount's hosiery factory on the left horizon. An ugly modern factory building on Nottingham Road now dominates this view.

Belper from the Parks: This scarce view of *c.*1930s shows the housing of Parkside, former Kiln Lane, in the foreground alongside Belper Parks. Nottingham Road lies behind with the gabled second National School (1910) clearly visible on the left. Just to the right is the well-known landmark The Windmill, dated 1796, on Windmill Lane with its castellated top, which has been tastefully converted into an unusual house, dated 1891. Park Mount, the distinguished gothic style house with apexed turret, dominates the centre skyline. This was the home of the Smedley family for many years. From the mid-1880s until the early 1900s, Mr Alfred Smedley lived at Park Mount. He was the managing director of Smedley Brothers Ltd, the manufacturers of steam engines and mortar mills. They were engineers, ironfounders and boiler makers and established their Eagle Foundry in Beckstitch Lane in 1858, originally for the manufacture of grinding mills. Eventually Alan Edward Smedley moved into Park Mount from Belle Vue Terrace. The apex to the house is now lost and the house is now boarded up for sale along with Fred Blount's hosiery factory complex adjacent on the right of this picture.

Bridge Street: This *c.*1906 view was taken from the corner of King Street looking northwards up Bridge Street towards Strutt's Mill. The street is alive with children and workmen. The poster board on the immediate right is headed W.L.& G.E.Neaum the auctioneers, whose premises were in Strutt Street and the poster is advertising the Belper Horse Show. The awning on the right is on the corner of Wellington Court. Today, the corner building still carries stone plaques dated 1852 and 1853. On the left stands a butcher in striped apron with his young assistant in white apron. The old Beehive Inn, with its globe-bracket lamp, is in the middle right and was run by Alfred Hazelwood in 1895; it ceased to be licensed shortly before 1911. On the opposite side of the road, the sign of the former Castle Inn is visible. This sepia image was almost certainly taken by C.W.Lee of Derby in a rare visit to Belper.

Bridge Street: This sepia illustration looking north up Bridge Street was sent on 10 August 1909 from Constance Allen at Riversdale, Bridge Street (Dr Allen's home) to a Miss Helen Jackson at Fernslope, Belper (Francis Joseph Jackson's house). The message reads: 'Will you come and have tea with us tomorrow Wednesday and go to the Horse Show? Come about 3 o'clock.' On the left are the marble and granite merchant's premises of James Beresford & Sons, with the George Hotel a few yards away. On the right-hand side behind the throng of Edwardians stands the well-established premises of William Samuel Bowler, chemist and photographic dealer.

Bridge Street: In 1905 Harold Burkinshaw took this extremely rare photograph of great historical interest from the top of Unity Mill chimney stack looking towards Strutt's Mill. The message on the back of this illustration reads: 'This is one of several views taken from the top of the Unity Mill.' It formed 'Belper Bird's Eye View No 1' from Burkinshaw's portfolio of views. It was sent from 'Frank' at Lime Tree Cottage, the 'Hibbert Homestead', situated on Long Row, Clusters Road, Belper, to a Mrs Hibbert Claremont, Shrewsbury, on 27 September 1905. Frank Hibbert was recorded as a Stationer at 32 Bridge Street. In the left foreground, at 61 Bridge Street, is the large house of Dr Richard Clayton Allen, the noted physician and surgeon, and Dr Richard Grammer Allen, medical officer for the Belper and Heage districts. The house, as now, was called Riversdale and is still a doctors' practice today. To the right is the roof of A.W.Altons & Co, grocer's, at 57 Bridge Street. On the middle left is the Baptist Chapel (1818 and rebuilt in 1893 with its Gothic turrets). Christ Church is top left before the mill chimney. Field Lane is clearly visible to the right, and the fire damage where Messrs Holden's furniture works were destroyed on 15 January 1905 can be seen to the right of Holden's three-storey warehouse building (now Greaves furniture store warehouse). The square-shaped Baptist Sunday School building is set back to the right of the fire damage. Behind here lies Joseph Street and in the distance, towards Matlock Road, the gables of Long Row School are visible. On the immediate bottom right lies Devonshire Terrace.

Bridge Street: This sepia view from the Kingsway Real Photo Series sold by W.H.Smith & Son was taken from almost opposite Christ Church Vicarage looking south down Bridge Street *c.*1913. On the immediate right stands the town's sub-Post Office run then by sub-Postmistress Mrs Mary Eley and which still exists today. Note the long wooden rake hanging from the wall to the right of the Post Office. Next door is the small fruiterer's shop of Fred Barnes. The horse and cart trundling southwards is about to pass the arched coach entrance belonging to the George Hotel run by John William Ashton. Prior to this, in the late 1890s, M.Tombin sold the Alton & Co's ales and wines and also provided luncheons and teas. The George Hotel was advertised as being close to the cricket and horse show grounds. On the middle left stands the old stone-built Belper Savings Bank (now Clusters Art Gallery).

Bridge Street: A young boy pushes his handcart and basket along Bridge Street *c.*1919 past the black and white half-timbered three-storey houses on the left called Devonshire Terrace. The ornate wrought-iron railings were removed to help the war effort between 1939 and 1945. The first gabled house on the immediate left is now used by the Woolwich Building Society (previously Refuge Assurance Co Ltd). The small pent roof at the end of the terrace is now the County Carpets shop. The gateway on the right leads to Riversdale, Dr Allen's house. The gateway entrance is now set back.

A GREAT ATTRACTION

REGENT HOUSE

Belper's Shopping Centre

DRAPERY AND FANCY GOODS

Keen Cut Prices for Cash

J. J. FOSTER, BRIDGE ST.
NEAR RIVER GARDENS

"EILEEN"
LADIES' & CHILDREN'S HAIRDRESSER.
APPOINTMENTS MAY BE BOOKED

Ye Old Arts and Crafts.

A SELECTION OF GIFTS AND ART LEATHER HANDBAGS.
The Ideal Shop for Whist Drive Prizes, etc.
Materials for Embroidery.

119 BRIDGE STREET - BELPER.

WALTER JONES
(Mus. Bac.)

PIANOS
BY ALL THE LEADING MAKERS
Easy Terms Arranged

BRIDGE STREET :: BELPER
Branches at Derby and Swadlincote

H. VARNEY

Joiner and Undertaker.

All classes of work undertaken in any part of the country.
Funerals and Cremations a Speciality.
ESTIMATES SUBMITTED FREE.

20 Bridge Street - BELPER.

TELEPHONE 78
C. E. GOODLIFFE
COMPLETE HOUSE FURNISHER
Unsurpassed in the District
For VALUE, QUALITY, —and GOOD SERVICE—
LOW PRICES
YOUR ENQUIRIES SOLICITED
BRIDGE STREET :: BELPER
Branches: Nottingham, Leighton Buzzard and Coalville

TELEPHONE 97
ALTON & CO.
(Proprietor: F. W. ALTON)
High-Class Grocers
WINE AND SPIRIT MERCHANTS
57 BRIDGE ST., BELPER

Advertisements for businesses in Bridge Street in 1928.

Wine merchant James Mellor Pym was established as far back as 1850 and by 1912 the firm had become James M.Pym & Sons, wine and spirits merchants and cigar importers, on Bridge Street.

Bridge Street: This early 1940s view looking north towards the East Mill was published by the Photochrome Co Ltd. The misspelt message to the rear reads 'Deer Dad, spent all Sunday afternoon on Derwent and rowed me up passed Ambergate opened country.' The corner of Field Lane is on the right and the corner building was Alan Newton's Associates Ltd, architects and designers, with the Rifleman's Arms public house sign visible further north along Bridge Street. The light on the left emanates through the gateway of Riversdale, Dr Allen's home.

Bridge Street: The Lion Hotel looks quite plain-fronted in this print from an old sepia photograph. In 1846, the Lion was recorded in *Bagshaw's Directory* as the Red Lion, managed by Chas Taylor, but was recorded in *White's Gazetteer* of 1857 where it was listed as The Lion Commercial and Posting Hotel (and excise office for the Inland Revenue) under the management of John Taylor; by 1888 Francis Bennett had taken over. Judging by the horse bus and the gentleman in the stove-pipe hat, this view must be *c.*1860s or 1870s period.

Bridge Street: This sepia view looking north up Bridge Street was issued by the Kingsway Real Photo Series in *c.*1913-14. The stone gate posts on the immediate left now lead to Thomas Ryde & Son, funeral directors, but in this view a sign advertises Holden & Sons cabinet makers. Next door was Mrs Maria Mee's fish shop (now Henderson's fishing tackle and countryware shop) and then Thomas Henry Fletcher's butcher's shop (now Rolo Blinds). Both shop windows appear to have hinged fold-out medieval-style display plinths. A fine open-top motor vehicle is parked outside the Lion Hotel which has by now gained a fine ornate wrought-iron porch and globe-bracket lamp. Mr George Sprey Harrison was the proprietor at this time. The adjacent wall and trees (right) indicate that the garage and car-park are not yet built. In 1903, when S.H.Hicks was proprietor of the Lion, it became the CTC's headquarters.

Bridge Street: The Lion Hotel has now received much refurbishment with pitched roof porch and little impediments (gables) over the upper windows. The Ind Coope signs are prominent in this *c.*1930s view. Motor car RB64 is parked outside the new motor garage selling 'Power' petrol at 1s 2d per gallon. During the late 1920s a masseur, Mr R.Myatt, used to attend the Lion Hotel each Wednesday and Saturday.

Bridge Street: This *c.*1910 view by well-known Derby photographer Francis Scarratt is looking north up Bridge Street. On the immediate left, Mr Beresford peers out of the doorway of James Beresford & Sons' family butcher's shop. The pillared porch of the George Hotel with its huge globe lamp has been a popular hostelry for years. The double upper bay windows on the right belong to Henry Gillett (late Snow) plumber, gas and hot water engineer. He was also captain of the Fire Station on Bridge Street. The people walking on the right are about to pass the narrow lane called 'Piggy Lane' after a slaughter house situated there. It may at one time have been named George Place.

Chapel Street: This sepia view of *c.*1920 shows the large brick-built premises of George Brettle & Co, silk and cotton hosiery manufacturers on Chapel Street. The factory was completed in 1835 and at one time was one of Belper's largest employers. In 1888 the manager was Mr Isaac Hanson who lived at The Woodlands, Belper, and he greatly improved the business. The owner, Sir Harry Twyford, sold the firm to Courtaulds Ltd in 1964. The building has been extensively altered since its closure in 1987 and is now known as De Bradelei House, housing factory shops and at one time Vistec's computer training office. In earlier times the firm was known as Ward, Brettle & Ward (Ward, Stuart and Sharpe & Ward were on Derby Road).

MAIN WAREHOUSE
SHIPPING
COUNTING HOUSE } CENTRAL 6564.

FANCY DEPT 115, WOOD ST
SPORTS COATS
SILK KNITTED SCARVES.
KNICKERS } CENTRAL 2105.

RETURN ROOM
35, GUTTER LANE. } CITY 3372.

ENGLISH GLOVES

"SUTOPLEX" (REGD TRADE MARK) FABRIC GLOVES.

TRADE B MARK

OBERON

"BELNIT" RIBBED UNDERWEAR MADE IN ENGLAND REGD TRADE MARK.

BRETTLE, CENT, LONDON.

119, Wood Street,
London E.C.2. 26.Mar.28

TO FACILITATE DELIVERY PLEASE ADD "G.P.O. BOX 129" TO ALL LETTERS, &C.

Miss Cooper RM. 36FE.

MANUFACTORY, BELPER, DERBYSHIRE.

Bought of
George Brettle & Co Ltd.
MANUFACTURERS OF
HOSIERY, UNDERWEAR & GLOVES AND WAREHOUSEMEN.

DEPARTMENTS.

COTTON, LISLE THREAD, SILK AND WOOLLEN HOSIERY AND UNDERWEAR.

GLOVES, UMBRELLAS & SUNSHADES, HABERDASHERY, CARDIGAN JACKETS, LADIES AND GENTLEMENS KNITTED SCARVES.

PLEASE ADDRESS ALL COMMUNICATIONS DIRECT TO THE COMPANY & NOT TO INDIVIDUALS.

DEPARTMENTS.

KNICKERS AND SPORTS COATS, SHIRTINGS, FLANNELS, BLANKETS, TOWELS, TABLE AND HOUSEHOLD LINEN, RAINPROOF COATS & MACINTOSHES.

SHIRTS, COLLARS, HANDKERCHIEFS, TIES, BRACES, DRESSING GOWNS, PYJAMAS, RUGS,

2/12	36	Job Merid Shirts	½S	38/-

This fine illustrated 1928 (designed 1912) bill head for George Brettle & Co Ltd shows an early engraving of their manufactory. The small building on the left is now the Orangery café and restaurant.

Belper Road (Derby Road): Regrettably, these ornate old houses with their gothic style gables and pinnacles have now been demolished. The beautiful houses with their many inset stone statuettes on their facia were former Herbert Strutt School houses, probably for their masters. The space left has been utilised as car parks for the adjacent Herbert Strutt School and former Railway Tavern public house. The Railway Tavern was run by Samuel Bryan and eventually by his wife Elizabeth from the end of the Edwardian era until at least 1928. It is now simply called The Tavern.

Babbington House: in 1857, Francis White described this building as follows: 'Large stone building, in the Elizabethan style, east of the Derwent on the Derby Road, and near the Railway Station.' It was erected 1838-40 on Babbington Meadows land which had been purchased from George Benson Strutt, who had proposed the building at a cost of £12,000. It was the Union Workhouse and was capable of accommodating 340 persons. Belper Poor Law Union consisted of 35 parishes and townships and had 53 guardians. The Union was divided into six registration districts – Alfreton, Belper, Duffield, Horsley, Ripley and Wirksworth. The average weekly cost of the indoor paupers during 1856 was (including rations of officers) 2s 6d each and, for clothes, 3½d. Chairman of the board of guardians was John Strutt Esq and he and the guardians met every Saturday at 10am in the Red Lion Inn (later Lion Hotel) on Bridge Street. This magnificent building with its gothic features was designed by Sir Gilbert Scott RA. In 1846 the workhouse contained 125 people and by 1857 this had grown to 205. During 1888 it contained 238 and by 1912, 340.

Babbington Hospital: Adjoining the Union Workhouse was a hospital built in 1889 at a cost of over £10,000, containing about 106 beds, the total accommodation being for more than 300 (G.H.Strutt gave generously once more). During World War Two it was refurbished and became an A1 Hospital under the control of the Derby Hospital Management Committee. Although a fine hospital, many Belper people were reluctant to be admitted because of its former associations with the workhouse. This aerial view by the Aero Pictorial Co Ltd was taken *c.*1940s and shows the extent of the many extensions and annexes since the previous illustration. In 1940 the governors of Herbert Strutt School secured from the board of guardians the use of the Union Chapel at a rent of 10s per week as an additional classroom for a sixth form group and by 1945 it became a permanent home to Form 1. The tennis courts are still in existence.

Babbington Hospital: This 1911 interior photograph shows the matron and her seven nurses in the gaslit Baron Ward which is situated in the main hospital block overlooking the tennis courts. There is an abundance of plants and flowers present, together with garland drapes (possibly for George V's coronation). The local chaplain can be seen on the right. This rare photograph was taken by Herbert Burkinshaw of New Road, Belper. Everything appears very neat and clean, especially the linen bedspreads and tablecloth. The stout man to the right of matron is probably one of the board of governors. He also appears later in the interior of Strutt's swimming baths so he may have been a doctor.

Belper Isolation Hospital: This second view of the hospital for infectious diseases gives a clearer view of the large central block with gabled three-storey central tower taken in 1907. The small construction near the base of the flagpole was presumably the kennel for matrons dog! The hospital is now a care centre for the elderly and many alterations have taken place over the last few years. The double-fronted, left-hand building is now flat roofed but the old lamp still remains. The message on the reverse side is from the former matron, Miss T.M.Gilborne.

Belper Isolation Hospital: Matron and her dog together with three nurses and a small child are pictured in 1910 outside the hospital situated off Crich Lane near to Ambergate and Ridgeway. The hospital was originally built in 1898 and contained 50 beds. In 1912 it was registered as Belper Joint Hospital District Isolation Hospital, Heage, Belper with Miss T.M.Gilborne as matron. The doctors Allen from Riversdale were the medical officers.

Derby Road: Motor car number UV3815 is parked outside Herbert Strutt's School in this *c.*19**50s** view looking north up Derby Road. The ornate gothic featured Lodge House to Babbington Hospital stands on the left.

The Triangle: This mid-1920 sepia photograph shows an early open-top bus coming from Ashbourne Road on to the main Derby Road. The Triangle was much smaller at this time but was later enlarged to contain flower beds, additional bench seats and two red telephone kiosks. Further alterations took place here to close off the left-hand slip road to Ashbourne, and the eventual installation of traffic lights. A small slip road still exists and is a useful place for parking. Christchurch and the Jubilee Clock Tower are on the left with the East Mill right.

Corner, Matlock Road: This rather empty scene of the Triangle is much earlier than the previous view and is probably *c.*1914. Note the fine iron lamp standard on the left outside the entrance to Christchurch. This gas lamp is numbered 121B on the glass. Note also the fine old 'To Matlock' cast-iron sign on the corner of the Triangle. A cannon from World War One stood on view at the Triangle for a short while.

King Street

King Street: This has always been Belper's most important street, running from the intersection of Chapel Street and Bridge Street uphill to New Road and the Market Place, with Jedediah Strutt's fine Green Hall residence at the top and entrance to the Railway Station at the bottom. Complete with the other notable buildings over the years - Palace Cinema and Theatre, the first Post Office, Council Office, banks, chemists and numerous public houses - it is still Belper's busiest street.

King Street: This view from an Edwardian postcard produced by George J.Jackson entitled 'Old Bridge, King Street, Belper' is actually a much earlier Victorian photograph *c.*1860s by an unknown photographer. The young boy with hand cart on the left poses with many others for this picture which is probably Belper's earliest-known photograph. Two of the old shops in the lower left were those of George Sheward (tailor and draper) and Rebecca Slater (milliner and dressmaker). Both shops are listed in *Bagshaw's Directory* of 1846 and *White's Gazetteer* of 1857. The buildings on the right were thatched. The ivy-clad bridge was commissioned by Jedediah Strutt II as a private walkway from his Green Hall Mansion - now Green Lane car park in 1832, just after the passing of the Reform Bill. The bridge led to Strutt's private garden (paddock) which is now the Memorial Garden and was removed in 1867.

King Street: This view from just below Green Hall looking down King Street towards Derby Road was taken by local photographer Harold Burkinshaw in *c.*1907-08. It was one of only a very few detailed photographs of the upper portion of King Street. The fine three-gabled and pinnacled building on the left is one of a fine architectural standard and still looks good today. The first shop is the ironmongers of Tranter & Hancox, with baskets, shovels, brush heads and sieves on display. The next shop is Boot's Cash Chemists shop with a draper's shop to the right. Freeman, Hardy & Willis Ltd, boot and shoemakers, are next with Hunter's the Teamen Ltd (grocer's) forming the corner shop on Strutt Street. The ornate turret towers on either side of Strutt Street are still a pleasing sight today. The twin gabled building to the right was a branch of the Crompton & Evans Union Bank Ltd, erected in 1881. In 1912 Thomas Tomlinson was the manager and the bank was open from 9am to 4pm except on Saturdays when it closed at noon. George Herbert Strutt purchased the old bank in 1922 and donated it to Belper as a war memorial. It is now the Amber Valley Borough Council Offices. Luke Booth's fishmonger's shop is on the immediate right and his 'catch of the day' is advertised on two chalkboards outside his shop.

King Street: A less busy scene than the previous picture. The Freeman Hardy & Willis overhead sign appears to have been replaced by a Public Benefit (a boot company) sign. At the end of Strutt's former garden on the left, half hidden by the foliage, stood a large enamel sign advertising Premier, The World's Standard Bicycle, and James's Cycles. The old lady on the right with her heavy shawl and head scarf is captured in the *c.*1909 view by George J.Jackson. (Note the large basket which appears to be full of some rather nasty gunge!)

King Street: Everybody stops for the photographer in this *c.*1906 scene. The large globe-bracket lamp on the left denotes the Midland Hotel with its large Strettons Fine Derby Ales sign above. The Waverley Café and Dining Room at 35 King Street were situated upstairs under the overhanging gabled roof, two doors up from the Midland. On the immediate right is John Ash's shop. Ash had pork butchers' shops in Days Lane and Queen Street between 1895 and 1912. Next door is the Imperial Vaults advertising Offiler's Fine Ales on the window. William Paxton's name appears as the manager and he was also recorded as a cab proprietor in Campbell Street. The first shop past the small alleyway (now leading to a pub garden) on the right was a tobacconist selling W.D.& H.O.Wills tobacco and cigarettes. Next was the London Central Meat Co Ltd, butcher's, with George H.Lumbley's draper's store next door. Peach's Commercial Dining and Tea Rooms/Temperance Hotel stood on the upper right, one shop down from the corner of Strutt Street, and was a popular venue for many Belper folk. The poster at the distant top right on the side of the Public Hall advertises a 'Venetian Fete' on Belper River Gardens, which was held on Wakes Tuesday, 1906.

King Street: The small boy on the right is standing outside a millinery and drapery shop, whilst next door is the well-stocked tobacconists of J.H.Bath selling St Bruno and Coral Flake. George Howarth, grocer and corn dealer, had premises where one sees the wooden upper structure (right) housing the warehouse hoist. The Midland Railway entrance to Belper Station is adjacent to the Edwardian pillar box on the left. Ball and Stillman's outfitter's and tailor's shop are opposite the hand cart and baskets on the middle right and advertised their expensive Burberry's clothes.

IF YOU WANT THE BEST RESULTS FROM THIS FILM RETURN IT TO BE DEVELOPED AND PRINTED BY–

CALVERT & SON

PHOTOGRAPHIC CHEMISTS

KING STREET :: BELPER

All Photographic work carried out Promptly

Advertisements for some King Street businesses in 1928.

DERBY GAS LIGHT AND COKE CO.

SUPPLY

GAS & COKE

IN THE

BELPER AREA

AT

DERBY PRICES

For Particulars of the Best Light and the Cheapest and Cleanest solution OF YOUR COOKING AND HEATING PROBLEM

apply at Branch Office:

King Street, BELPER

TELEPHONE 36

King Street: This *c.*1926 view looking up King Street towards the Market Place is dominated by Dick's shoe shop on the corner of the cobbled entrance to the Railway Station. The proprietors of the business were Hart's Footwear Ltd. The upper portion of this famous shoe shop window is dominated by the advertisements for 'Wigwam' moccasins for women (price 24s 9d and 29s 9d). Another advertisement says, 'Wend your way in Wigwams'. On the right three motor cycles are parked near the railway bridge and boot makers and repairers of H.E.Clay & Co at 28 with the old wooden hoist cabin of Howarth's the miller and corn merchants still *in situ* above. William's Deacon's Bank Ltd is adjacent at 34.

King Street: This *c.*1915 view looking along King Street towards Bridge Street is taken from the vicinity of Peaches Hotel and Café. The entrance to Belper Station is on the right; the wrought-iron balustrade above Ball & Stillman's clothier's, outfitter's and tailor's shop at number 30 is on the left. The Liberal Club was situated above the shop. The fine building with its arched entrance at the corner of Campbell Street is that of the National Westminster Bank at 20. The horses and cart are outside Howarth's the miller and corn merchants.

King Street: This *c.*1930s view is taken from the end of Chapel Street looking up Bridge Street with the mill chimney in the distance. The fine arched windows and columned frontage of the Midland Bank, built by the local firm J.W.Haynes of Strutt Street, stands on the corner of King Street. Mr J.R.Davis, the manager at this time, was also treasurer to Belper Rural District Council and to the Union. Women dominate this sunny day in Belper with over 20 ladies in view, all wearing highly fashionable hats. The accountant's firm of Oswald Ling, Greaves & Co, were housed in the Midland Bank Chambers. To the left of the bank, a large advertisement for G.Bishop, high-class English and foreign fruiterer is evident.

King Street: This *c.*1930s view is looking up King Street towards the Market Place. At number 3 stands the Home and Colonial Stores with its enamelled sign above the window. The billiards and snooker sign on the left is that of the Derwent Club, kept at one time by Wilf Fisher. The archway entrance to the billiards room was the scene of an accident when a certain Major took his horse through when it reared up and killed him. The former Palace Cinema and Theatre stands at the bottom right, now Wilkinson's hardware store. The early 1930s silent films featuring Tom Mix, Eddie Polo and Pearl White were shown here, entrance fee 2d.

King Street: This is an early production from the Artistic Postcard Co of London, number 2551 chromotyped in Saxony, and is taken from the lower part of King Street near the Rose and Crown public house (shown on the immediate right and selling John Smith's Gold Medal Tadcaster Ales and Stout). This *c.*1906 view clearly shows the stone building on the immediate left with its arched doorway and railings prior to being refurbished by G.C.Brittain's the printers. Next door stood a tobacconist's shop.

Established 1870 Telephone 53

G. C. BRITTAIN & SONS LTD.

THE HOUSE OF TRUE VALUE

General and Commercial Printing

Wholesale Stationery, Toys and Fancy Goods, Wrapping Papers, Wallpapers, Paints and Distempers, Paper Bags, etc.

Wholesale & Retail *Quotations Submitted*

KING ST. :: BELPER

(OPPOSITE THE PICTURE PALACE)

King Street: This is an early 1920s view looking up King Street from the Palace Theatre. G.C.Brittain's printers, booksellers, bookbinders, stationers, paper merchants and toy dealers premises are on the bottom left. Established in 1870, the firm was previously in Bridge Street. The draper's shop of Stanley Thomas Clay stands left at number 17. A little further up King Street is the Railway Hotel public house, formerly the Tiger Inn which was run for many years by Miss Hilda Bradley and then Mrs Mary Bradley. The façade of the Railway Hotel is now an ugly modern design. The Belper Freemasons of Beaureper Lodge number 787, whose secretary was Tom Brown (a printer), used to meet in this hotel. The Rose and Crown pub stands right, run by Robert Green at this time. It was on the present site of Boots the Chemist.

King Street: This fine *c.*1919 photograph by Frederick Holbrook was produced from his George Street studios in Belper. Much bunting together with UK and American flags are evident on both sides of King Street. To the right is the old Palace Cinema and Theatre. Clarkson Rose, the famous ventriloquist, used to perform here. The scene is dominated by hundreds of young girls and women parading from the top to the bottom of King Street. The precise details of the event are unknown but it maybe some sort of Sunday School parade to celebrate victory in World War One.

Market Place: This publication is from an early drawing or painting, possibly by Frank Beresford, Belper's notable artist. Behind the fountain stands the Angel Inn which was thatched in this turn-of-the-century view. In 1895, Mrs Martha Millward was the proprietor. A foul murder was reputed to have occurred within these premises. The inn has since been demolished and a Salvation Army citadel has replaced it. Most of the other buildings here have also been demolished, including the King's Head Inn to the right of the Angel Inn. A message on the front of this illustration, addressed to Mrs S.Edwards of 28 Albert Street (Samuel Edward's house) states: 'Annual meeting of the L P A A, 1 July 1916. Belper Wesley School. You are respectfully invited to the Tea at 5pm.'

Market Place: This slightly faded sepia photograph was taken by George J.Jackson of the Butts *c.*1908. On the immediate left is the ornate brick and stone premises of Charles William Southern, chemist and druggist. Over the doorway and windows the signs denote 'Established over 50 years', together with a sign beneath the name of Southern denoting 'Kiddy and Ashton'. We know that Samuel Kiddy ran a chemist's shop here in the early 1840s and 1850s. In 1895, Southern's were also listed as mineral water manufacturers and their various pot and glass bottles are highly collectable today. They were also wine and spirit merchants. Their sign over the doorway, 'Patent Medicines, Reduced Prices', was a well-known feature. Some older Belper inhabitants may remember a larger sign spanning the whole of the premises and proclaiming 'Southern's Food for Infants' in the early 1920s. The ornate lower frontage of this famous chemist's has now been modernised for Belper's new Market Head video store. Next door is the premises of wholesale grocer's, the Bakewell Brothers, now part of Colledge's furniture store. Across the small yardway stands Waterloo House and John Burton's millinery shop. They were destroyed by fire and demolished as part of road widening, Colledge's have their later premises built here. On the immediate right stood the large prestigious premises of George Barringer grocer, wine merchant and provision dealer. Mr Barringer (in the bowler hat) and his assistant can be seen in the doorway with his horseless cart parked outside. The signs denote that he was an agent for Robinson & Co's Burton Ales and W.& A.Gilbey's wine growers and distillers (10,367 1st bottles mentioned on this sign!) Next door is Jones & Co draper's. In the centre stands the well-established stone building of the White Swan public house. The arched doorway and left-hand window now have later replacements. Along with many others who have noticed the presence of the photographer, a young delivery boy smiles with his basket under his arm.

Market Place: In this *c.*1930s midday photograph by Lilywhite Ltd of Halifax, people on the left are staring into the shop window of Loverock & Son, draper's and outfitter's, which has in recent times become the Victoria Wine Stores. On the right stands the three-storey arched windowed drapery premises of J.William Walters at 6 Market Place. This was previously called Compton House. The elegant features of this building are now lost to the modern facia of Hayne's furniture shop. The neat tree-lined garden at the top of King Street has in recent times been replaced by a new block containing a domestic appliance centre and solicitors.

Market Place: This clear black and white *c.*1915 photograph by Frederick Holbrook looks down from the top of the Market Place, right down King Street to Bridge Street. The exterior bracket clock face of John Medley's watchmaking premises on King Street clearly shows the time is 11.45. J.G.Bosworth & Son's butcher's shop and house dominates the right-hand side of the picture at the commencement of High Pavement.

Belper Market Place: This elaborate memorial outside J.& G.Bosworth butcher's shop is from an undated and unknown photographer's work belonging to Mrs Olive Burdekin. A wooden or cardboard covering has been placed around the waterless fountain and surrounded by about 60 jars of fresh flowers and many wreaths in remembrance of the 'Glorious Dead'. The plaque reads: 'The Blood of Heroes is the Seed of Freedom.' The view is thought to be *c.*1947.

Market Place: This 1909 view by the well-known Derby photographer Francis Scarratt of Abbey Street shows some young Belper children hanging around the market stalls at closing time, possibly awaiting a small payment to dismantle the stall displays. The outline of the old thatched Angel Inn is in the background.

Telephone 82

BOSWORTH & SON

M. A. BOSWORTH & W. KNIGHT

High-class Family Butchers

QUALITY, SERVICE, SATISFACTION

Wholesale and Retail

Market Place and Bridge Street

BELPER

S. ORME

MUSICAL INSTRUMENT DEALER

Pianoforte Tuning and Repairs a Speciality

Gramophones and Up-to-Date Records always in Stock

TEACHER OF MUSIC

Your Enquiries are earnestly Solicited

Note the Address:

3 MARKET PLACE :: BELPER

Advertisements for Market Place businesses in 1928.

Market Place: This 1897 sepia photograph (almost certainly by Frederick Holbrook but not confirmed) has captured Belper's contribution to the Diamond Jubilee celebrations for Queen Victoria's 60 years of reign. A brightly decorated platform has been erected in front of Walter L.Loverock & Sons' drapery store on the Market Place while hymn singing is orchestrated from within. The 30-strong band play beneath the platform and hymn number one on the programme is about to commence. Thousands of Belper's inhabitants turned out for this important occasion and, as was usual for this period, they all wore hats. This photograph came from the Stevenson family and James Henry Stevenson (dyer) is believed to be on the platform with other notable locals and clergy.

Market Place: Engineers and workmen are engaged in the erection of Belper's waterless fountain in 1881. The sturdy timber framework and simple rope winch were used to good effect. Several older Belper folk have taken a particular interest in the activity, depicted in this reprint from an old photograph. Water was never connected to this monument. The waterless fountain is inscribed: 'Erected by the inhabitants of Belper to commemorate the paving of this Market Place by G.H.Strutt Esq and dedicated to the use of the public, 4 July 1881.' The single gas lamp at the top has since been replaced by two modern lamps and an iron flower or plant basket. Much of the Strutt solid stone paving is now covered in ugly tarmac.

Belper Fair: The exact location of this fair is unknown. However, a brief message on the reverse side of this scarce photograph reads: 'Belper 1906'. W.Cross' 'Stud of Ponies' ride dominates the scene in front of a building with arched windows which may have been a chapel. Most of the ponies are taken up by white-smocked girls, the boys preferring to pose for this unknown photographer. In the background a sign reads: 'W. Cross's Steam Circus' and behind the boys lies 'The Greasy Pole'. The scene may be somewhere near the Coppice off the Market Place which was the traditional site for fairs.

Empire Day: This appears to be a small private party to celebrate Empire Day (which was on 24 May) possibly 1911. Everybody has dressed in their Sunday best for this scarce scene taken by Harold Burkinshaw. The round canvas awning was made by F.J.Thomas, Chertsey, Surrey, and is decorated with pictures of King George V and Queen Mary. A large 'Welcome' sign is close by with another 'for the Empire'. A large plate of bread and butter is on the table and several people and children are wearing Empire Day medallions. The exact location is unknown but hopefully someone will be able to advise the author. 'One King, one Flag, one Fleet, one Empire,' so Britain boasted in the days when the sun never set on her possessions across the globe and the map was full of red.

High Pavement: This view of the Nag's Head Inn is one of the sepia-printed publications of the late 1930s/40s by F.Frith & Co Ltd of Reigate. The widening of High Pavement took place in 1911 and substantial stone walls were demolished, the stone being utilised to form the existing wall seen here on the left. The original Nag's Head public house sign can be seen on the right. Joseph Watson was the landlord throughout the 1840s and 1850s. Others recorded were Mrs Eliza Shaw in 1888, Samuel Kittle in 1895 and Albert Day in 1912. An early 1890s advertisement in the time of Samuel Kittle proclaims: 'Belper Norfolk Brewery. Home Brewed Ales. Small casks supplied at moderate charges. Dinners provided at the shortest notice.' Other businesses in the area of High Pavement included John Roads, a shopkeeper in 1912, nearest to the Nags Head *which was latterly a toffee shop*; Mrs Eleanor Wilder, draper at number 9 (top right of picture) selling ladies underwear. The house in the lower left was that of Mrs Brenda Sanders (née Lee) who had a fruiterer's shop at the front. Her father was known as 'Sooty' Lee, an apt nickname for his occupation as a chimney sweep.

HAROLD BARNES

HIGH-CLASS
Baker and Confectioner

TRY OUR BREAD

CONFECTIONERY FRESH DAILY

Parties Catered for

THE BUTTS BAKERY - BELPER

Market Upholstery Works

(Proprietor: E. W. TAYLOR)

Wholesale and Retail Manufacturers.
Dining and Drawing Room Suites.

All Classes of UPHOLSTERY Executed.
Stuffover Work a Speciality.
Estimates Free.

THE BUTTS, BELPER
DERBYS.

Advertisements for businesses on The Butts in 1928.

The Butts: The 18-strong band and 40 plus soldiers of the Belper Volunteers muster on The Butts during the late 1890s. On the immediate left are the corner railings of the Park Tavern. The house and shop on the top left were those of Walter Johnson the cycle maker, now a photographic shop. The premises on the right were those of 'Cloggy Wass'. W.C.Wass & Sons were clog and boot makers. The lane on the top right leads down to Parkside. Many years ago, every 31 October, cattle markets were held on The Butts.

The Butts: The Butts offer beautiful views of the Parks, New Breck and the sweeping hillside of the Chevin. This scene by an unknown Victorian photographer came from the Stevenson family, the dyers and dry cleaners in Belper. The Butts corner public house and terraces are all beautifully adorned with garlands and flowers to celebrate Wakes Tuesday *c.*1897-98. The Butts are situated a short distance from the Market Place up the steep hill of High Pavement. It used to be the site of many cattle fairs and the Friday statute fair where local worthies could hire servants during the 1860s. The Butts were famed for their ornate well-dressings and teams were formed each year to carry out this intricate and worthwhile handywork, often during the Wakes celebrations. The Belper Volunteer Regiment and other local militia used to muster on The Butts. The corner building was the Park Tavern public house and in 1895 George Cholerton was the licensee with a beer-only licence. The Park Tavern was often referred to by locals as the Corner Pin. Percy Wilmot was landlord here for a while. The Park Tavern has been demolished enabling Lander Lane to be widened. A well-kept green stands in front of these listed buildings. St John's Chapel is out of view in the top right corner. Many small businesses were once situated in The Butts area. Some examples are: Harold Barnes (baker) at 27; Lee & Co (grocer's); Henry Fletcher (patent medicine vendor); James Melbourne (beer retailer); Joseph Gregory (wheelwright and carriage builder); Morley Payne (beer retailer); Joseph Haynes & Sons (grocer's); Clifford William Scott (confectioner); George Julian Jackson (photographer); William Edward Taylor (upholsterers); Walter Johnson (cycle maker); W.C.Wass & Son (boot and clog makers); Frederick George Lodder (boot repairer); John Reader (baker); Horace Looms (builder); John Mellor (clothier and draper); Jas Akers (shopkeeper) at number 22.

FULL WEIGHT SOAP—

John of Gaunt Cleanser,

3d. per pound.

HAYNES & SONS,
The Butts, Belper.

"John of Gaunt, with helm and lance, did ride,
Or practised with his archers on the Butts."

Joseph Haynes & Sons of The Butts, Belper, advertised their new full weight soap – the 'John of Gaunt Cleanser' – far and wide. This 1908 advertisement was placed on the rear of a postcard of Caversham Lock and the soap was sold at 3d per round. The legend relates to 'John of Gaunt with helm and lance did ride, or practised with his archers at The Butts'.

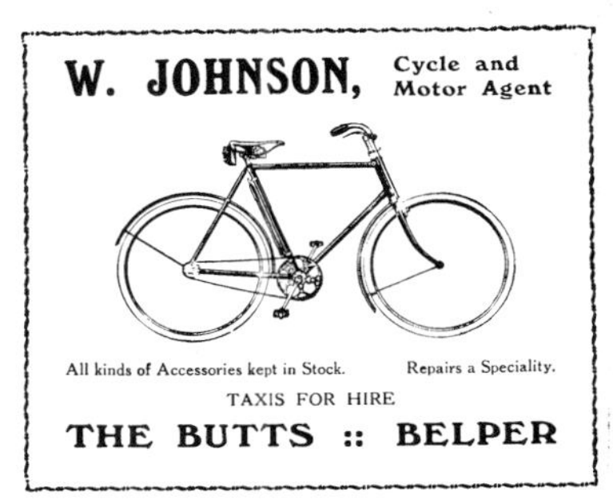

Advertisement from 1928.

Belper Grammar School: This view was specially published as a postcard for the school and shows the side view of Belper Grammar School House. The message on the reverse side is addressed to J.C.R. Le Marques Esq and reads: 'It will be best for you to travel by the Midland Railway from St Pancras as Belper is on the Midland. Signed GMW.' A message on the front reads: 'If you will let me know what time you arrive at Belper on Monday, I will try and meet the train. Yours faithfully G.Mellor Wright.'

George Mellor Wright was the headmaster at the time this postcard was posted in January 1907 and he was recorded there in 1912. The Grammar School was first established in 1841 and enlarged in 1903. Mr G.Vale was the headmaster then. The *Court Guide* of 1903 refers to the house and school buildings as being 'Lofty, well ventilated, especially designed for school purposes with an excellent system of drainage, and a water supply which a recent analysis has pronounced to be unsurpassed for purity. All the sanitary arrangements have been carried out under the direction of a first-class firm of sanitary engineers. The rooms are well-lighted, warm, and furnished with all modern appliances. For illustrated prospectus containing terms and full particulars apply to Headmaster, G.Mellor Wright (formerly senior master of New College, Margate). Assisted by an efficient staff of resident and visiting masters.'

One of the school's early advertisements reads: 'The school, old established and well known, is pleasantly situated on the main road from Derby to Matlock about two minutes walk from Belper Station. Convenient trains for school hours from Derby, Matlock, Duffield, Shottle, Whatstandwell, Ambergate and Butterley.' This private grammar school on Chapel Street eventually closed and was taken over by Derbel Manufacturing Company and is now Brettle's factory shop.

Green Hall: This hall was situated on what is now Green Lane car-park. This fine building was erected in 1810 as Jedediah Strutt II's private residence. (Green Lane was formerly known as Jedediah's Lane and then Market Street Lane.) The architect for Green Hall was thought to have been William Strutt. It is not certain when the Strutt family left Green Hall, but certainly by 1888 it had become a private preparatory boarding school for young gentlemen run by Miss Sophia E.Taylor. She was recorded here through to 1895 and beyond 1912. An early 1903 advert stated: 'Green Hall, Preparatory School for Sons of Gentlemen. Miss Taylor, assisted by efficient masters (University men) and Governesses, prepares boys for Public Schools (ages from 7 to 14). Scholarships gained direct from Green Hall to Repton School, St Columba's College (Ireland), Derby School, St Paul's School (London) etc. Green Hall, standing in its own grounds, occupies an elevated position in the pleasant part of the town, and is within five minutes walk from the Railway Station.'

General Smuts, the prominent leader of the Boers, was in his younger days a teacher at this school. The hall was requisitioned as a military convalescent hospital during World War One. At some stage in the mid-1920s a school clinic was held here and a Miss Daisy Catherine Hughes was the nurse who attended on Thursdays (2pm-4pm and 10am-12 noon for infants' welfare). After World War Two the hall was divided up into flats and eventually demolished in the late 1950s to become the present car park.

Belper nurses: The George Street photographer Frederick Holbrook recorded this rare scene of nurses taking time out for a game of cards. Pencilled on the reverse of the card is the simple message, 'Green Hall W.W.I. Convalescence Hospital'.

Beecholme College: This was another of Belper's private schools and was situated at the top of Orchard Street off Green Lane. It was established in 1889 and recognised by the Board of Education in 1903. The principals were the Misses Norman, assisted by resident certificated governesses, visiting masters and mistresses. One of its early advertisements in 1903 stated: 'The College, which is within five minutes walk of the Railway Station, stands in its own grounds in a lovely and healthy locality, and has extensive tennis lawn and playgrounds. Terms and full particulars on application to the Principals.' This old house was formerly the home of Isaac Hanson, the managing director of George Brettle & Co Ltd. Prior to the private college being established in 1889, Isaac was recorded in 1888 as residing at the Woodlands and this name is still inscribed on the gate posts today. By 1895, however, Mr Hanson had moved to Lumb Grange and Ebenezer Smedley moved from Brooklyn Villa, Chapel Street into the Woodlands. The message on the reverse side reads: 'To Miss D.G.Beastall, Somercotes Hill, Alfreton. I got this from Miss Norman (Principal) this morning. With love from Nellie.' Prior to Beecholme, the Misses Norman had been at Belle Acre Terrace and Bridge Street.

Beecholme College: This fine Burkinshaw photograph was sent to a Mrs Liby Sherriff, Clairmonte, Tylers Green, High Wycombe, Bucks, in June 1912 and reads 'Miss Norman and myself wish you every happiness in your future life. Much love and best wishes for fine weather'. This view gives a clear view of the magnificent gate and gate posts leading to Beecholme College, The Orchard, Belper.

Long Row Schools: The Strutts (Jedediah's sons William and Joseph) built the original Long Row Mill Schools not far from their factory. They were Lancastrian Schools where, by 1846, approximately 500 children, including the infant school, were educated for a penny per week each. A Sunday School of 400 children was also held in the same room, entirely supported by the Messrs Strutt. The schools had spacious playgrounds. The Long Row Schools were erected in 1818 for 200 boys, 130 girls and 200 infants. In 1888 the average attendance was 175 boys, 170 girls and 140 infants. James Tomlinson was the master, Miss Frampton the mistress and Miss Mary Anna Nodin was the infants mistress. The School Board purchased Long Row Schools in 1887 and the school was enlarged in 1895 for 228 boys, 310 girls and 207 infants. By 1912, Charles Bint (formerly of the Pottery School) was the master, Miss Lee the mistress and Mrs M. Nicholson the infants mistress. George Jackson took this important photograph of local school life which includes 129 boys and five ladies. The boys all have short hair, 16 have their arms folded and only two are wearing their caps. There are not many smiles either in this *c.*1906 scene at the bottom of Long Row on Bridge Street corner. The boys' school was the lower school, infants in the middle and girls were in the upper school.

Long Row Schools: This rare illustration of 'Santa Claus' laden with gifts was produced by Harold Burkinshaw in 1906. He attended the poor children's Christmas tea given by the readers of the *Belper News* at Long Row Schools on 28 December 1906. Each of the approximately 600 children present received a toy. The illustration was given away free with the first edition of *Belper News* in 1907. I wonder how many copies have survived.

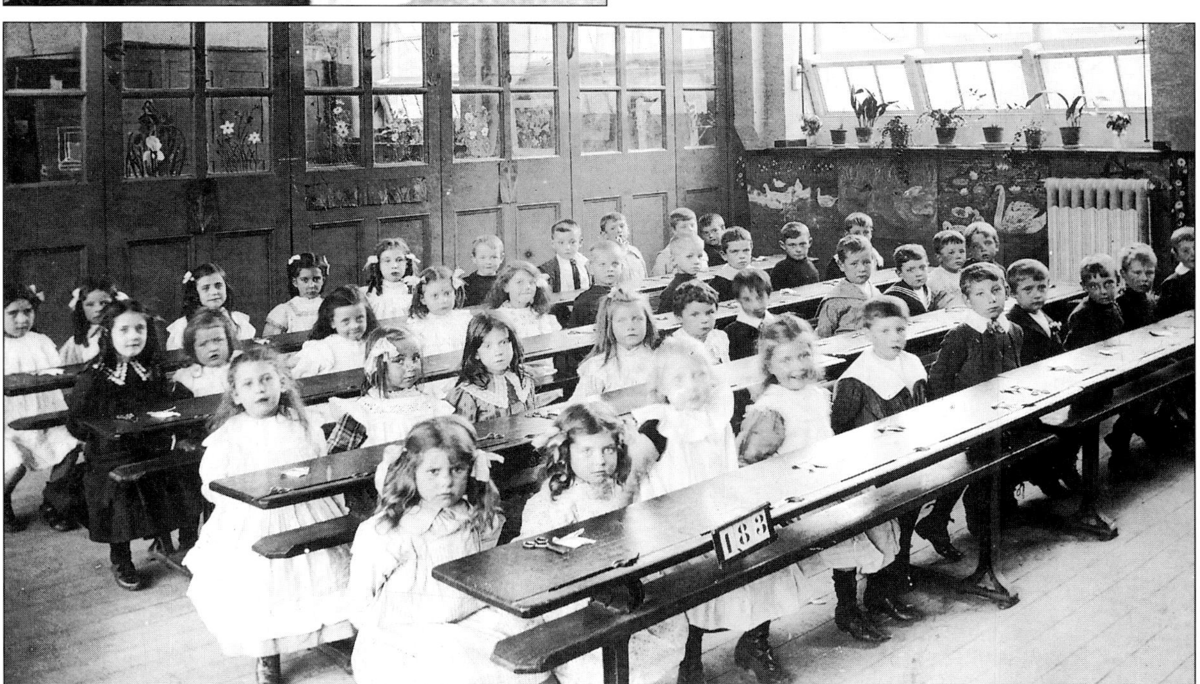

This mixed infants' class of 22 boys and 18 girls is thought to have been photographed *c.*1909. The photographer is unknown but the illustration came from Miss Emma White of 5 Joseph Street, Belper. It is difficult to see what subject they were being taught, but each has a folded piece of paper and a pair of scissors. Could it be the proverbial schoolroom paper aeroplane under construction? The folding centre screen was typical of many schools around the Belper area, such as the Fleet School and St John's School.

Belper School: There is just the occasional hint of a smile in this carte-de-visit style photograph by T.B.Mellor of Belper. This class of 58 girls with their stern-looking mistress on the extreme right of the back row is believed to be the Pottery School. Note the segs in the girls boots.

The Fleet School: One or two cheeky grins are evident from Class VI of the Fleet Boys' School in this 1911 school photograph, commissioned from Harold Burkinshaw. The Fleet School was built in 1882 for 300 boys. The average attendance in 1888 was 90, when Peter Whitfield Jones was the master. The 1895 edition of *Bulmer's Directory* records: 'It consists of one large room and two class rooms, having a total accommodation of 164 which is wholly occupied.' The 1912 *Kelly's Directory* records the average attendance as 95 when Daniel Wilson was the master. In this class of 36, only nine are without their flat caps and, for some reason, are all placed at the right-hand end of this group photograph. Note the large dicky bow on the boy in the middle of the front row, sixth from the left.

The Pottery School: This charming group of 36 school girls, part of The Pottery School Belper, was taken by an unknown photographer *c.*1905. This was a Board School, being a large brick building erected in 1877-79 for 140 boys, 160 girls and 150 infants. The *Derby Mercury* of 1878 reported that the Board fees for attendance would be '7d for girls and boys over seven years of age, infants 2d per week and part-timers 3d'. There were many complaints from the lowly paid in Belper. By 1888 the average attendance was 130 boys, 120 girls and 95 infants. Charles Bint (later of Long Row School) was the master, Miss Edith Ellen Brooks the mistress and Mrs Sarah Alton the infants' mistress. *Bulmer's Directory* of 1895 confirms that the school had accommodation in the three departments for 444 children with an average attendance of 390. In 1890 the school was enlarged to take 170 boys, 160 girls and 175 infants, and by 1912 the average attendance was 160 boys, 150 girls and 155 infants. J.H.Brocklehurst was the master at this time, Miss C.Parkin the mistress and Miss Clara A.Shenton the infants' mistress.

National School: This is Belper's original single-storey National School (St Peter's) built in 1849 on The Butts, Nottingham Road, at a cost of £1,000 raised by subscription and a grant of £536 from the National Society. It was a neat stone Gothic building and consisted of one large room, 80ft x 70ft, divided in the centre by a wooden partition and accommodated about 400 children. The average attendance in 1857 was about 150 boys and 130 girls. In 1888, William Adderley was the master and Mrs Hannah Anthony the mistress. This reprint, from an old sepia photograph, shows up to a dozen pupils probably on a day off *c.*1900. In 1910-11 the school was demolished and rebuilt in two storeys to accommodate 300 boys and girls (the average attendance was 280) and renamed St John's School. It was once called the Church of England School. Peter W.Jones was the first master of the new National School.

Boys' school: Harold Burkinshaw took this group shot of 14 extremely smart boys in their suits and striped caps. We are not sure why the young boy on the front left is wearing an ordinary flat cap, as is their master. They are probably from a private school, perhaps the Green Hall Preparatory School for Sons of Gentlemen.

Strutt School and Public Baths: This view of the school is taken looking south and shows the corner of Gibfield Lane. The notice board advertises evening classes. The Herbert Strutt Public Baths with the huge glass roof built in 1910 are on the left with the inscribed stone plaque 'Herbert Strutt Baths 1910'. The building in view to the left was the baths superintendent's house at one time. The Public Baths were erected at a cost of £9,000 which was defrayed by Alderman George Herbert Strutt DL JP. The baths comprised of a swimming bath 68ft x 20ft and two foot and six slipper baths. There were 47 dressing-boxes.

Herbert Strutt School: Two Edwardian children on their way down Derby Road stop for Francis Scarratt's photograph of Herbert Strutt's Higher Elementary School at midday in 1910. The gothic style building was chiefly constructed using local stone from the Strutt quarry at Makeney and built on the Turnip Pingle and Plantation site belonging to Mr Strutt. Designs were by the Belper firm of Messrs Hunter &Woodhouse, whilst the builder was J.K. Ford of Derby. The total cost was £15,000 and Alderman G.H. Strutt DL JP, chairman of Derbyshire County Council defrayed the entire cost. The school at this time was managed by nine governors, and the principal was William Wright Tunnicliffe BSC (LOND) FCS, who remained headmaster from 1909-1936. He was followed by George Ducker MCBA. The school was opened on 8 May 1909 by the Duke of Devonshire. It contained a central hall, nine classrooms, art room, laboratories, dining hall and could accommodate 200 scholars and 30 pupil teachers. There was also a cookery and manual training centre. Messrs James Beresford & Son executed the provision of a memorial to George Herbert Strutt, made of Carrera Marble and mounted on a pedestal of green Genoese marble. It was unveiled in the school house by Colonel G.Gascoyne on 5 January 1910.

High School: G.H.Strutt provided three additional classrooms and a fine dining hall, cloakroom and an art room in 1916. The school could then accommodate 400 pupils. The extension can be seen on the right with the new arched wall jutting out from the gothic clock tower turret in this R.Sneath photograph. The message on the reverse side reads: 'This is a photograph of the New Herbert Strutt School, don't you think it a fine building?' Over the years the school gained in reputation for its achievements. In 1941 it had 250 pupils enrolled in the Air Training Corps and in 1949 established a branch of the Combined Cadet Force. In 1974 it became a middle school, but by 1986 it was a junior and infants school only.

The Herbert Strutt Baths

GIBFIELD LANE
BELPER

Under the management of the Belper Urban District Council

These Baths are open from April to October each year. Facilities for Ladies and Gentlemen and also for Mixed Bathing

Apply to the Baths Office or to the Urban District Council for Schedule of prices and times

THE

Herbert Strutt School

BELPER

This School, founded by Ald. G. Herbert Strutt in 1909, provides a sound High School Education for Boys and Girls up to the age of 18.

A Preparatory Department has been opened for pupils between the ages of 8 and 10.

There are excellent Laboratories, Art Room, Gymnasium, Cookery School, Library, Dining Hall and well-furnished, well-ventilated Class Rooms.

Prospectus with full particulars may be had from the Headmaster, who is always pleased to interview parents by appointment.

G. T. TERRY, *Solicitor,* **Clerk to the Governors**

Herbert Strutt Public Baths: Harold Burkinshaw took this *c.*1913 photograph showing the Belper Police Swimming Club. Don't they look a grand sight in their all-in-one bathing attire? These swimming baths hold fond memories for many locals who remember that people could dive in but that jumping in was not allowed. The superintendent in 1912 was Arthur W.Stapleton and by 1928 William Marsh was in charge. The baths have been boarded up out of use for some time now. One assumes that George Herbert Strutt would not have approved the closure. He presented the baths to the Belper UDC on 27 April 1910. In the deed of gift, he stated:

'...but so nevertheless that the scholars for the time being attending the said Herbert Strutt Higher Elementary School shall have the right to use the said swimming bath without any charge for so doing except for the use of towels and clothing on two days every week.'

Belper Territorials: This pair of extremely scarce photographs shows the Belper Territorials in the area of the Clusters, Belper, not far from the Old Drill Hall which was erected in 1902 at a cost of £2,000 by George Herbert Strutt. The pictures were taken by Frederick Holbrook of George Street, Belper, prior to 1915. In the first view, the young Army officer struts down the line inspecting his men. Note the two Army cyclists with their rifles strapped along the cycles' crossbars. Many local Belper people young and old turned out for the occasion. 'F' Company of the 5th Battalion, Sherwood Foresters (Notts & Derby Regiment) used to meet at the Drill Hall in Clusters Road. Some notable names were Captain W.H.Christy-Clay, the medical officer Lieutenant G.B.Gill MB, RAMC (TF), and Colour-Sergeant Clement Walker, the drill instructor.

This sentimental card from World War One was produced by the famous greeting card publishers Wildt & Kray. The message on the front – 'When shall I see you again at Belper?' – must have been said by many Belper womenfolk as their loved ones went to war. This publication was posted August 1916.

This unknown soldier's photograph, taken by Fred Holbrook, came from the Stevenson family (dyers) and may well be one of their family.

The Sherwood Foresters' flag is unfurled in a Belper church. This is another production by F.Holbrook, who must have had a monopoly of photographs associated with World War One.

Memorial Gardens: Situated opposite Green Hall in Upper King Street, the present day Memorial Gardens were the former private gardens of Jedediah Strutt II and he held tea parties here. The grounds were often referred to as his paddock, and bands played here. The Memorial Gardens now contain an obelisk of Cornish granite erected in memory of Belper men who fell in World War One. Their names are inscribed on panels at its base. The site was presented and the memorial unveiled by George Herbert Strutt Esq VDDL JP. This early 1950s view shows Green Hall on the other side of King Street a few years before its demolition. The fine old cedar tree is now much larger and is in excellent condition. There was a good turnout for the service to mark the 50th anniversary of VE Day, held in the Memorial Gardens on Sunday, 7 May 1995.

This card was offered by ex-servicemen for sale to help them during the uncertain times after leaving service and being unable to find employment after World War One.

Ex-Soldier's Appeal.

NO PENSION. NO DOLE.

Credentials produced if required.

Can you give this Ex-Serviceman a Job or help him by buying this Card?

It is just a simple story
That I want to tell to you,
Yet, in spite of its simplicity,
It is alas, too true.

When I saw that I was needed,
I enlisted full of pride;
They said I was a hero then,
But now I'm cast aside.

I have tramped along the highway,
I have searched each city through,
But good luck never comes my way,
I can find no work to do.

So now you know my story,
I ask you if you can
To try and spare a trifle
For a poor Ex-Serviceman.

Funeral Parade: The three views featured here, taken from a series of photographs originally issued as a set of four by Frederick Holbrook of George Street, show that hundreds of people turned out for this unknown funeral *c.*1917. Boy Scouts of all ages are marching in the funeral procession or watching from the sidelines. Many of the Scouts will be the Belper (1st) Christ Church troop (Mrs G.H.Strutt's own), where the Revd H.S.G.Walker BA of Christ Church was the Scoutmaster. The first picture is thought to be part of King Street. The extremely large turnout may indicate that this was a Strutt family funeral.

Strutt Street: The fine stone and brick building of the main Post Office dominates this *c.*1911 view of Strutt Street looking towards King Street. George H.Roulson was the postmaster at this time. Judging by the open windows and the open tunic of the postal worker standing outside, it must have been a hot summer day! The PO has now ceased to function here and is now on the opposite side of the street, while this fine old building is now the Jehovah Witnesses Kingdom Hall. The British Legion building has since been built in the gap to the left. The Farmhouse Fayre Café lies in the gabled building four houses towards King Street. George Jackson took the photograph and the message on the reverse side reads: 'Thought you might like a postcard of my new abode. This, by the way, does not flatter it. Pleased to say the office is OK. Kind Regards, Banks.'

This 'pull out' type postcard entitled 'A man of Letters from Belper' contained 12 different Belper scenes and was posted in 1913.

Lucerne Villa: This fine three-storey bay-fronted house with stone balustrade above is the end house of two on Derby Road (the other is Sherwood Villa), and has 'Lucerne Villa' inscribed in the stone gate pillars. It was built in 1885 by John Smedley. The following residents are recorded: 1888, Norris Cowin; 1895, Thomas Elrick (commercial traveller); 1927 C.B.Tranter (of Tranter & Hancox). The beautiful gate is now lost with the gateway entrance bricked up. The wall to the right has gone to make way for a garage. The small lane and terraces of Meadow View are to the right, out of view. These were built by the Smedleys (Eagle Iron Works) for their foremen.The house now belongs to Mrs Clutterbuck (née Smedley), a former local councillor, who was the first Lady Mayor of Belper in 1978. It is named Lucerne Villa because the first owners honeymooned at Swiss resort.

Somershall House: This 1920s scene shows a young lady wearing a straw boater, with what appears to be the Herbert Strutt School crest on it. It is probably her sister in the pram on a sunny day outside of Somershall House on Derby Road (now number 43). This large house with its neat lace curtains formed part of a row built by Laban Brown, the builder, also of Derby Road. This house was the former residence of Frank Stillman. Both Frank and Maurice Stillman were part of the long-established Ball and Stillman, clothiers, outfitters and tailors at 30 King Street, and a shop bearing their name still exists in Campbell Street today. The house was turned into two flats approximately 30 years ago, and in 1995 has undergone a facelift; the ornate wooden balustrade has been removed, the bay-windows have been replaced and the top stories of the wall removed by Simon's Joinery and Building Contractors.

Gibfield Lodge: This grand stone-built house is situated on the corner of Gibfield Lane and The Avenue which runs parallel with the railway cutting. Several Midland Railway Co cast-iron marker posts still line The Avenue along the top of the embankment today. Gibfield Lodge was built *c.*1893 and thus could not .have been the lodge house to the former Gibfield House which existed approximately 40 years prior to the existence of Gibfield Lodge and probably disappeared at some time before 1904. The residents of the former Gibfield House are recorded as: James Oldham Sweetenham, attorney and steward of manors in the Fee of Duffield in 1857; Jas Edward Murphy LDS, 1888 (Revd Edward Murphy was a Wesleyan superintendent in Albert Street by 1912); Edward John Hadderton Hoskyn LSA LRCP LRCS, surgeon and physician 1895 – he lived on New Road by 1913.

Gibfield Lodge was at some time in its life connected with Methodism, and was a a manse the equivalent of a vicarage or rectory. The message on the reverse side of this card reads: 'Services are here at 5 and 8 tomorrow and as 8 would be an awkward time because of school, I intend going at 5am, Isn't it early!' It is signed 'M' and was sent to a Miss Haynes in Leek and posted on 24 May 1906. Former recorded residents here are: John Cheetham (auctioneer), 1912; Frank Holden, 1927.

A local story relates that in the 1920s a cobbler used to use the side path to reach his workplace and lodgings which were the old damp stables in the rear garden. The stone balustrade and ivy are lost and a garage exists to the left, but the house and garden still grace this part of Belper. Gibfield Lodge now belongs to Dr Morrissey and family.

Watergates: Harold Burkinshaw took this fine view of Watergates in 1909. This large house is situated in the Shottle-Ashbourne road, close to Blackbrook, and stands in its own grounds with lovely country views. The stone entrance porch is inscribed 'J.E.P.' and the iron rainwater pipes are dated 1907. The house was built for Joseph Edgar Pym. The house has a 'twin', The Rise, not identical but by the same architect, situated adjacent and built for another member of the Pym family. J.E.Pym formerly had a house in Bridge Street in the late 1890s. The message on the reverse side of this particular card reads: 'Wishing you a very Happy Xmas and Bright New Year from Mr & Mrs Edgar Pym, 1909.' The house with its sturdy entrance doors look much the same today, but now has ivy clinging to the front. The name Watergates is thought to have derived from the old ruined farm on land at the rear of the house.

Burndale: Henry Mellor sits with his dog on the garden seat inscribed 'Burndale' for this early 1920s view taken by Frederick Holbrook. Burndale House is still situated on Pingle Lane and now has wisteria growing up it; a modern bungalow now sits to the right. The original Burndale sign on the front of the house still exists. In 1912, Henry Mellor lived in Acorn Lane. The message on the reverse side of this card reads: 'Uncle Henry Mellor's House, Belper.' A John Henry Mellor had a successful baker's business at 76 Bridge Street from *c.*1910-1930. Henry Mellor was a churchwarden at St Peter's Church in 1924.

Private garden: This early Burkinshaw photograph records workmen constructing a wooden framework and thatch for a garden summer house somewhere in Belper. The actual location is unknown, but may have been on Bridge Hill or Ashbourne Road. The garden is very large and has a flag-pole in the centre.

Builder John William Haynes (senior), his wife Ruth and J.W.H. (junior) proudly stand outside their neat double-gabled house on Strutt Street. 'Jack' Haynes established his building contractor's business in 1900 and it ceased trading in 1983. Young John William, seen here in his sailor suit, eventually took over the reigns once his father died in the early 1950s. The right-hand room became the general office and the left-hand room was at one time rented out to Derbyshire County Council (a police sergeant resided here). Eventually the house was completely used as an office, where Dennis Hough worked diligently for 47 years. The Haynes family made several noteable contributions to Belper's architecture: extensions to Herbert Strutt's School including fireplace memorial; built the Bank of Scotland (former Williams Deacons) premises in King Street; built the Midland Bank premises in King Street; built St Swithun's Church on Cow Hill (The Fleet); converted King Street Public Hall into a cinema. This house pictured above has now been demolished and the site is now occupied by the new Co-operative Society store. Harold Burkinshaw was commissioned for this photograph in 1908. The original postcard was sent to Nurse Edwards on Albert Street (Miss Clara Edwards). J.W.Haynes owned several houses in Belper and a Mrs Robinson of Mill Lane remembers having to go through the large gates in order to pay the rent.

Field Lane: This is another of George Julian Jackson's fine sepia photographs of *c.*1914 looking up Field Lane from Bridge Street corner, close to the former house and studio of local artist Frank Beresford. The eight neat bay-fronted terraces have been built on the site of William Holden & Sons' former workshops destroyed by fire in 1905. The cab further up on the left stands outside the shoeing and general smiths premises of Albert Wigley, previously a blacksmith in Wellington Court off Bridge Street. The premises have since become occupied by J.Allen & Sons car hire, motor hirers and funeral car suppliers. By 1927 Albert Wigley was running the Field Lane smithy whilst Mary Wigley was shoeing at Wellington Court. Today, 12 Field Lane is called Blacksmith's Cottage. The sturdy wooden gateway on the left used to lead to Holden's warehouse which now belongs to Greaves, the Belper furniture store.

Field Lane: Scot, Russell & Co of Birmingham's 1905 publication clearly records the extent of the fire damage to Messrs Holden's furniture works on Field Lane which occurred on 15 January 1905. William Holden & Sons had their cabinet-makers shop on Bridge Street (now Greaves furniture store). In Victorian times they were also furniture removers and had a business in Derby. The message from 'Ada' in Belper to 'Minni' in Marehay, Ripley, reads: 'This is the ruins of the workshop.' Bridge Street is visible on the bottom left of this picture, where Lloyds the chemists exist today.

Holden's workshops: This extremely scarce photograph by an unknown photographer clearly shows the extent of the damage. The man on the left with the flat cap, standing with the fireman, is believed to be one of the Holden family. The fire chief with his polished helmet surveys the disaster area. Ironically, the fireman on the extreme left (nearly out of the picture) appears to be holding a pipe.

Advertisement dated 1928.

Albert Street: This view is the bottom right-hand side of Albert Street *c.*1910-11 and was posted from 24 Albert Street on 15 April 1911. Number 24 is to the left of the old gas lamp, whilst Rose Villa is still clearly visible, its name inscribed in the tall arched entrance to number 28, to the right of this view. The end house with the arched upper window is number 26, The Laurels, and this was the former residence of James Francis Stevenson, the master dyer and cleaner, after he moved from Derby Road some time after 1912. The stone balustrades above the bay windows of numbers 26 and 28 are now lost. However, a pair of ornate cast-iron window boxes are still present below the upper windows. All the railings were lost to the war effort between 1939 and 1945. Over the years many successful Belper men have lived in Albert Street. Next door, at number 28, the old brass bell-push is still *in situ* today.

Laund Hill: This local amateur photograph is of Laund Hill, Belper, and the short row of sturdily-built brick houses are numbered 15, 17, 19, 21, 23, and 25 from left to right. The first arched entrance to the left is that of Nezereon House, now painted out. Up to seven people are in the garden on the right peering over the walling. Both the stone and brick walls are now lost to enable cars to park. Laund Nook Farm is not far away and on the Far Laund, a toll gate existed, being pulled down in 1797.

Midland View: George Jackson took this *c.*1910 photograph not long after the sturdily-built terraced houses of Midland View were built in 1909. 'Midland' obviously referred to the adjacent Midland Railway Co. The narrow lane and line of houses running parallel with the railway cutting below are known locally as the 'Bowling Alley'. Lewis Edward Gell, an electrical engineer, lived here in the 1920s and stables were to be found along here. A small council depot, a former Smedley foundry, also existed, where disinfectant could be acquired. Number 12, the second house, is now a barber's shop. In 1995 Belper locals were dismayed at an attempt to rename the lane 'Railway Terrace'.

Methodist football team: This photograph of Market Street Methodists FC, posing in front of their makeshift goal netting, was taken by the sisters E.& G.Wayne, photographers listed at King Street. The ball denotes that they were champions of the Belper & District Sunday School League probably *c.*1911-12. The man squatting on the right with dicky bow and trilby wears a black arm band (hopefully not an omen of the match result).

This team belong to an unknown Belper football club, and again the photograph was by E.& G.Wayne, this time taken in 1913-14. The ball appears to have the inscription 'RBFC'.

The Meadows: This view of The Meadows, Belper, was published by Lilywhite for John Halifax, a newsagent of 38 King Street, and was taken in the late 1930s. The view formed part of a nine-view composite selection of Belper. A lengthy message was penned on the reverse side, some of which reads as follows: 'My Dear Miss Isabel, How splendidly you did at the Connington Sale and I hope St John's is a success. You will have seen in the *Belper News* Mrs Greenwood and Mrs Coupland had died and today Mrs Roulson (*of Albert St, wife of George Henry*) has been laid to rest. She has been a invalid for a long time with heart trouble but was out in the car Friday and died Saturday. Yes Dr Alan (*Riversdale*) thinks I look well, I got weighed at Calvert's (*a King Street chemist*) and am 11st 4lb, so you may still laugh. With love, Naomi.'

Belper Horse Show: This is 'Optimistic', a well turned-out trotting pony at the Belper Horse Show in the 1920s. The photograph was taken by Stanley Thomas Clay, who was a draper of 17 King Street. The 1928 *Belper Official Guide* (price 3d) states that the Belper Horse Show, held in August, 'was always an interesting event and largely attended'.

Belper street game: Those ornate iron railings with their scrolls and points are a fine piece of work that would cost a small fortune today. The young Belper lad 'about to bat' is captured by photographer George Jackson in this *c.*1908 scene in an unknown street somewhere in Belper. One clue is the right-hand basement window where the possible shop advertisement appears to be for 'Rowntree's', and also the *art nouveau* tiles below the right-hand ground-floor window. The magnificent inscribed gate posts and their pinnacled tops have hopefully survived, but the railings were probably lost to the war effort. The portable wickets were a good idea for setting up a game and certainly saved making chalk marks on the fine stonework.

Belper outing: This 44-strong group are outside the Dog and Partridge Hotel at Thorpe near Ashbourne. Harold Burkinshaw took this fine photograph on 20 June 1908 and produced it at his New Road studio. Some interesting statistics are: ten bowler hats, eight boaters, nine flat caps, seven pipes, four cigars, two umbrellas and eight walking canes. Nearly everyone has very fancy buttonhole flowers, on this special day out for the men of Belper. It is possibly a Methodist group outing as the photograph came from the Stevenson family (dyers) of Belper.

Belper outing: This superb early photograph shows many Belper people on a day's outing to Tideswell in *c.*1910. The 58-strong group are lined up outside the stone church of St John's which was a cruciform building belonging almost exclusively to the Decorated style of the latter half of the fourteenth century. Many noteable Belper people are depicted here alongside the Marquis of Granby coach. It was obviously a men-only outing, although at least one lady was involved (right). Many of the faces are the same as those outside the Dog and Partridge at Thorpe in the previous illustration.

Alfred Tomes ironmonger's: This *c.*1920s photograph was thought to be Alfred Tomes' ironmonger's shop somewhere in Belper. The original postcard came from Belper. However, Alfred Tomes was always situated at 56 Bridge Street. This scarce photograph clearly shows the many items for sale at the time *eg* mangles, dolly tubs, sieves, buckets, mops etc. It is now thought that this would have been Alfred Tomes' first shop prior to him moving to Belper. Possibly it is in the West Midlands area.

Belper exhibition: The occasion is unknown, but may have been a display for an exhibition. The tea cup and saucer looks out of context in this unusual view taken by Harold Burkinshaw *c.*1910. The various items include a small musical instrument, stool, heavily studded chair, small carved figures and three crude axes. The author would be pleased if any further light could be shed on this unusual collection.

The thatched style summer house stands in the left background and the magnificent shell fountain with cherubs has started to form a distinct pool in the grass. Beneath the shell lie three gruesome but intricate entwined fish. The maid stands obediently in the background for this *c.*1913 Burkinshaw photograph. The exact location is not certain. A large brick building with corrugated type roofing appears behind the trees.

Belper children: Frederick Holbrook took this photograph of two unknown Belper girls in his New Road studio. The long-haired fairies were probably going to a fancy dress parade.

An open air pageant with some excellent scenery is captured in this 1907 scene. The stage set to the right denotes the scene is outside "The Old Barley Inn" . Judging by the smiles and the overspilt washing basket it may have been a farce!

This picture was part of an old stereoscope card and shows two unknown Belper boys dressed up. The tricycle has a horse's head and is decorated with flowers.

Chapel Street resident: This charming scene *c.*1911 by a local photographer has the words 'Tommy Green, Belper' written on the back. Presumably he is with his grandchildren sitting outside his terraced home on Chapel Street. An Arthur Thomas Green was listed in the 1912 *Directory of Belper,* at Chapel Street and again at 27 Chapel Street in the 1928 *Directory*. He must have lived to a ripe old age.

Amateur dramatics: The girls in the white dresses all have 'fairies' wings and at least two of the young boys are wearing several medallions and ribbons. The other elder ladies all sport fans or parasols in this local production of *The Mikado* taken by Birkinshaw *c.*1908.

Ambulance Corps: This clear black and white picture was taken by an unknown photographer. The message written on the reverse side is from 'C at Chapel Street, Kilburn 11/11/09' and reads: 'This is a photo of our Ambulance Corps at Belper, it was taken on Hospital Sunday when we were sheltering from the rain in the Public Hall. I expect Olive will pick out Mr Jackson.' The Public Hall is a plain edifice of brick erected in 1882 by a limited company at a cost of £3,500 and consisted of two principal halls, the larger holding about 650 persons and the other 250. It also contained a council room and other offices for the officials of the Urban District Council. Petty Sessions were held here. The non-uniformed men standing at the rear are supporting the huge banner of the twentieth century Equitable Friendly Society, register No.1047 London, 'Friendship and Truth'. In this 1909 scene the hall had *art nouveau* style wallpaper and was lit by gas.

Conservative Ball: Everybody faces the photographer in this interior scene of the 1907 Conservative Club Ball held at the Public Hall on King Street. The picture was taken by Harold Burkinshaw of New Road. The Conservative Club on Campbell Street is an edifice of local stone built in 1888 at a cost of £2,000 and in 1912 it included billiard, reading and committee rooms plus a residence for the steward and had 190 members. By 1928 membership had risen to 260. The land for the club was denoted by George H.Strutt, who became its president.

Liberal by-election: Harold Burkinshaw captures the Liberal candidate for the 1914 Derbyshire North-East by-election. He is precariously balanced on the narrow window ledge behind the wrought-iron balustrade spelling out Ball & Stillman's outfitters' and tailors' shop. The Liberal Club was situated in the upper portion of their premises on King Street. Old and young alike stare up to listen to the politicians pearls of wisdom. Many of the men puff on their pipes and the ladies, especially, appear to be extremely well dressed. The two stocky moustached policemen are there to control the proceedings. Only four of the women in this picture are without hats.

The Thorn Tree Inn: This inn was situated on Field Head (now Chesterfield Road) on the corner of Swinney Lane. This extremely rare interior view of the Thorn Tree Inn bar was taken by Harold Burkinshaw *c.*1911 and depicts a delightful scene where the landlord, Mr John Alton, and his family compose themselves for the photographer. The bar surface area shelvings are heavily decorated with many flowers and ferns, possibly celebrating the coronation of George V in 1911. Everything appears to be to hand: old-fashioned bottle opener/cork screw close to Mr Alton's son; match holder/striker near the hand of the poker-faced customer (one assumes he must be sitting down). Today the ornate bottles and flasks on the mirrored shelves would be a collector's dream. The shelving remains but the ornate bar is no longer, but may be covered up under panelling. During the late 1920s and well into the 1930s, an Edward Tomlinson was in charge. He was a beekeeper and his nickname was 'Belgium Bill'. Whiskey, gin and rum were tuppence-halfpenny a tot, brandy 3d and Guinness 5d. Another landlord was William Walker (1888-1895). Charles Wilmot in his 1894 book entitled *Belper and its People*, wrote: 'Looking back to when the Cemetery opened in 1859, Swinney Lane was opened up as a public thoroughfare crossing the Chesterfield Road at Field Head. And here at the angle of the roads is the Thorn Tree Inn where years ago grew a large thorn tree. This property was once owned by one Thomas Smith, whose maternal ancestor was known as Betty Knocker. She used to sell pegs at 3d each from her house and gave each customer a pint of ale. Later the beer business was transferred from her home to the Thorn Tree Inn.'

Cattle fair: From the early 1880s and probably earlier still, fairs were held in Belper on 12 May and 31 October and for hiring servants on 1 November. By 1888 fairs were held on 28 January, 5 May and 31 October for cattle, and by 1912 the cattle fairs were held only on the last Thursday in October. This continued up to 1928. This *c.*1916-17 photograph by Frederick Holbrook shows a good turnout for the cattle market. The man in the centre in an elevated position holding the stick is presumably the auctioneer. The well-to-do and working class are all present in readiness to make their purchases. In the background, the tower of St Peter's is evident in this view of the cattle market held at this time to the rear of the Lion Hotel and garage.

Alton & Co advertisements: Alton & Co's Derwent supply stores were established in Bridge Street during the late Victorian period. From 1912 through to 1928, Alton & Co's grocer's business was recorded in Kelly's *Derbyshire Directories*. The supply stores were situated opposite the Devonshire terrace houses on Bridge Street. Alton & Co were agents for this early chromo-litho advertising card for Dr Tibble's Vi-Cocoa, sold in 6d packets or 9d and 1s 6d tins. Vi-Cocoa was advertised: 'To give the hesitating wheels of life glibber play. The price of ordinary Cocoa, but Ten times its value.'

Belper Park: This extremely rare photograph came from the well-known Stevenson (dyers) family of Belper. It depicts a huge 1902 Coronation celebration for Edward VII on the Park. There must be many hundreds of Belper people in this picture and every person, young and old are wearing hats, mostly straw boaters. The band has mustered in front of the stand on the right where the many Belper dignitaries are situated. This scene needs to be studied under a magnifying glass. The Salvation Army ladies with their bonnets can be picked out along with soldiers and Salvation Army men. Many people appear to be holding programmes or song sheets. Note the old man with a stick, sitting with his back to the proceedings behind the stand, presumably enjoying some shade from the day's sun. Many locals watch from their doorways and upper windows on Parkside. If you look carefully you can see that the whole site has been set out with numbered pegs and string. One of the houses in the background has a large portrait of Edward VII over the doorway. New housing has since been built on the other side of Parkside. Certain of the houses on Parkside former Kiln Lane have been built using vivid Red Accrington bricks making them stand out from others.

Belper's Railway: The original North Midland Railway engineered by George Stephenson was completed in 1840. It was constructed in a deep cutting to avoid alterations to Belper's well-established roads and streets. Within the space of approximately one mile, ten bridges had to be built to carry the streets and roads over the railway cutting. The original station at Belper was situated a little under three-quarters of a mile south of the present station with its entrance off Derby Road. It was designed by Francis Thompson and had many stone arches and was of the Italianate style with a parapet roof. In 1878 it was replaced by the present two-platformed station built in a narrow cutting and opened on 10 March that year. Situated nearer to the town than the original station, its entrance is off King Street. The second station cost £2,806 2s 11d and was built by John Greenwood.

Belper Station: This photograph looking north towards Ambergate was taken by Harold Burkinshaw *c.*1910. Eighteen milk churns are evident between the two platforms. The slipway on the right with the neat wooden paling fence is the entrance off King Street. The first bridge in view carries Field Lane. Six people await a northbound train on this sunny day. Note the lower quadrant mechanical semaphore signal with its white backboard so that it is not obscured by the bridge. All the smart buildings on either side of the station here have now been demolished. Alas, the smart railway benches and well-kept flower beds would not survive today.

Belper Station: Some 15 years or so later, the scene is little changed. The fencing is newly painted white and there are still several milk churns on view. The southbound steamer is about to stop for the 20 or so locals to climb aboard. The old gas-lit platform lamps appear to be intact but some of the signs have been changed from wood to cast-iron. During the early 1930s there were special Bank Holiday trips to Blackpool. A return ticket before 9am cost 15s, but was reduced to 5s after 9am.

This interesting page is reprinted from the 1928 *Official Belper Guide* when the local rates were 13s 4d in the £ and electric lighting was charged at $6^1/_2$d per unit.

BELPER

(DERBYSHIRE)

Accommodation. HOTELS: Lion, Bridge Street (R.A.C., A.A.); Railway, King Street. REFRESHMENTS: Cadena Café, Bridge Street (see page 4 of cover); Waverley Café, King Street (see page 4 of cover).

Area: 3,119 acres.

Market Day: Saturday.

Early Closing Day: Wednesday.

House and Estate Agents: Claude Willder, Chapel Street, Belper; Godfrey Ford, The Mart, Belper.

Banks: Midland Bank Ltd.; Westminster Bank Ltd.; Williams Deacon's Bank Ltd.; Belper Savings Bank.

Newspaper: "Belper News and Derbyshire Telephone."

Population: 12,329 (1921 census); now estimated at 13,500.

Post Office: Chief Office—Strutt Street.

Public Services: Gas, 2/11 per 1,000 cubic feet, 7d. per therm; motive and manufacturing power, 2/6 per 1,000 cubic feet (see page 35); Electric Light, per unit, light 6½d., power 3d.

Rateable Value: £66,236.

Current Local Rates: 13/4 in the £ (1928).

Distances by Rail

	MILES.		MILES.
Burton	10½	Matlock	9
Derby	7½	Nottingham	12
Leicester	35	Sheffield	28
LONDON	134	Stafford	39

Distances by Road

	MILES.		MILES.
Ashbourne	12	Duffield	3
Bakewell	18	LONDON	138
Burton	19	Matlock	10
Chesterfield	20	Sheffield	30
Derby	8	Uttoxeter	24

Belper omnibus: The inspector (right) and his young assistant appear to be resting on an old wooden handcart before their next journey. Bus RA 371, belonging to the Poundall Brothers of Belper, appears to have a nearside rear dent. Poundalls were a small firm operating with eight or ten buses. The family had a well-established butcher's shop on Nottingham Road. The Poundalls used to run a friendly local service from Strutt Street to Shottle Gate via Belper Lane End and other diversions. They would pick up and deliver parcels and even take shoes to the cobblers. This service was known as 'Shottle Emma'. Percy Poundall also used to have a small lorry to help people 'flitting' (*ie* moving home). The story goes that his lorry could not pass a pub. Mr & Mrs Blount recall that when they moved from Belper to Ambergate, Percy first called at the Park Tavern on The Butts and again at the White House on Toadmoor Lane.

Accident on New Road: This large traction engine came to grief in *c.*1910 and ploughed into the side of the Black Swan hotel and public house, formerly called Nether Swan and later Wine & Spirits Vaults. The globe bracket lamp advertises the Black Swan wine vaults whilst the left-hand board advertises Alton & Co mild and bitter ales. Walter Neaum was in charge at this time and was later followed by Harry Ryde. It looks as if the left-hand front wheel may have come off and caused the accident. Various engineers survey the disaster, watched by interested locals. A general provisions shop advertising Oxo and a tea blenders stands to the right. The *Telegraph* coach running between Chesterfield and Derby used to change horses here.

Ring up No. 30 Belper.

THE DERWENT GARAGE.

CHAPEL STREET, BELPER.

OPEN AND CLOSED CARS FOR HIRE NIGHT OR DAY.

Moderate Charges. *Every description of Repairs.*

Proprietor:—H. SELVEY.

Derwent Garage: Note the old telephone number 'Belper 30' in this late-1920s advertisement for the Derwent Garage, Chapel Street, Belper, then near to Woolworth's and the Trent bus depot. Horace Selvey was the motor engineer at 13 Chapel Street. The old-fashioned wedding scene was to attract potential customers to hire their open or closed cars. This item was a giveaway advertisement with blotting paper backing. Horace Selvey was killed on Burleigh Hill near Quarndon.

Sam Smith's Motor Car: This 1907 scene depicts a remarkable piece of Belper's social history. The view is believed to be on Nottingham Road, Belper. The two unlikely 'worthies' are Sammy 'Peg Leg' Smith and 'Lavender'. It is alleged that Sam Smith lost a portion of his leg in an early motor vehicle accident. As a result he constructed this 'Heath Robinson' type motor car out of old wood and wheels to form a cart that he could push around. He also devised a rather odd-shaped walking aid to assist his passage. He apparently sold boxes of matches and postcards from his 'trolley'. Once they were married the penny postcards were pre-printed with the following legend: 'I'm married now I'll let you know, I've married quite a fairy, Some people call her Lavender, but her proper name is Mary.' You can see one of the postcards on his near 'flag pole' Mary's nickname was due to the small bunches of lavender that she sold from Sam's motor car. Lavender was Joseph Haynes' daughter from their grocer's premises on Lander Street.

The Chevin: Walter Beardall of 16 King Street took this delightful and peaceful scene on the Chevin some time after World War One. The lady in white with her walking stick (possibly Mrs Beardall) sits on the neat stone wall of the adjacent farm whilst two farmers (one carrying a pail) stroll up the lane towards Swiss Cottages. Richard Dale was a farmer on the Chevin for many years. The farm on the right was known as Swiss Farm and the farmhouse as Swiss House and that to the right Chevin Green Farm. A Mr John Burton, a draper in the Market Place, lived at the Swiss House on the Chevin in 1895.

Kilburn Road: Another scarce sepia photograph by an unknown photographer looking up Kilbourne Road (Kilburn) in 1909. The Meadow Cottages of 1912 on the right still look good today. The three young people on the right are outside what is a present-day newsagent. For many years previously Ernest Alldread and family ran a newsagent's from here. Ernest was easily recognisable by the patch over one eye. The open hedgerow to the left has now been overtaken by a series of modern semi-detached houses. The large house on the top right dominates the brow of the hill and still exists today. The hill was called Bedlam Hill and is often referred as that today by Belper locals. In the distant right, the inn sign of the Seven Stars public house in the district of Barton Knowle is just visible. At this time Thomas Spencer was in charge. In 1888 a beer retailer, Samuel Spencer, was operating in Openwoodgate.

Openwoodgate: This small hamlet is situated on the Kilburn Road out of Belper. This fine photograph by an unknown photographer is a rare piece of topographical history relating to the little photographed Openwoodgate in 1909. In the centre is the beer retailing business (now the Spinning Jenny public house) of John W.Patchett advertising Alton & Co's mild and bitter ales and stout from their Wardwick Brewery in Derby. Parked outside where a sign advertises stabling are what at first appears to be three loaded horse and carts. However, the animal in the centre with large pointed ears looks more likely to be a mule. A sign denoting Sandbed Lane is on the wall behind Howarth's the butcher's. The handsome Bull's Head public house run by John Parkin stands on the left of the picture and still sells Kimberley Ales today. The girl on the right with white shawl and large umbrella smiles outside the grocer's, draper's and Openwoodgate Post Office, all run by Mrs Harriet Mills. This later became Arthur Millward's grocery shop. Both this view and the previous view were posted to a Mrs Taylor, Mill House, The Chevin, Belper, in December 1909. Other businesses in the Openwoodgate area were: George Chidlaw, fried fish dealer; James Jackson, shopkeeper; Arthur Millward, grocer; Herbert Wain, fried fish dealer; George Fred Howarth, pork butcher.

Ambergate Introduction

A wide picturesque stretch of road from Belper leads into the village of Ambergate, the 'Gateway of the Peak' where road, river, rail and canal meet and run parallel for some distance through the Derwent Valley; with Alderwasley Woods on the west side and Crich Chase on the east side.

The River Amber, four miles long, an affluent of the River Derwent, joins the Derwent near here.

In 1895 Bulmer's *Directory of Derbyshire* described Ambergate 'as a prosperous village and important railway junction, situated about 2½ miles from Belper. Many good houses and shops have been erected and there are extensive saw mills and lime works and a wire manufactory. The surrounding scenery is varied and beautiful.' Few rambles of the county excel in sylvan beauty than that from Ambergate station to Cromford or Matlock. Romantically situated at the confluence of the Derwent and the Amber, in 1926 Ambergate was immortalised by an unknown poet with the following: *A story told in simple rhyme, I in these lines relate, Of two who went to Paradise, By way of Ambergate.*

Ambergate was partly situated in Heage and partly in Crich parish. The township of Heage was formed into a parish from the civil parish of Duffield in 1844. Francis Hurt Esq, of Alderwasley Hall, was Lord of the Manor in the 1840s.

The manor anciently belonged to the Ferrers family and was later annexed to the Duchy of Lancaster. Heage parish was under the management of a Local Board from 1863, but was succeeded in 1895 by an Urban District Council. Prior to the railway opening in 1840, Ambergate was of little importance, but went on to have three new stations over the next 36 years.

In the main the growth of the tiny hamlet of Toadmoor from being just a few scattered stone cottages consisting of the odd nailer, cowkeeper and boot repairer was entirely due to the building of the North Midland and the Buxton, Manchester, Matlock & Midland Junction Railways.

Ambergate became so important for people travelling the railways that the following ticket sale statistics are recorded: 1872 - 28,207 tickets bought; 1882 - 56,000; 1892 - 63,157; 1922 - 90,157.

The success of the railways brought other businesses and employment to the area when George Stephenson and the Clay Cross Co introduced their Lime Works in 1841. As a result of the railways and lime works, the sparsely populated area of Toadmoor/Ambergate increased its inhabitants to 206 by 1851. The year 1876 must go down as one of Ambergate's most important dates. This was when the unique triangular station was constructed, and the former Thatched House Tavern Commercial Hotel and Posting House closed, being converted into three cottages for use by the Midland Railway (Now Nos 1, 2 & 3 Midland Place). Francis Hurt, because of the closure had the Hurt

This is the oldest known photograph of Ambergate, dating from *c.*1897, and shows the scattered hamlet of Toadmoor. In 1895, T.Bulmer's *History, Topography and Directory of Derbyshire* referred to this area as follows: 'Toad Moor is a hamlet almost adjoining Ambergate, which will at no distant date lose its identity in the younger and more prosperous village.' It is hard to believe that the main A6 road to Matlock now runs along the bottom of this view. The brick terraced houses on the lower right adjoining the White House on the main road are just under construction. Almost all the old stone houses cling to the winding formation of Toadmoor Lane with just a few on Newbridge Road. The large thatched farmhouse shown here in the centre is now lost. The entire central area now contains many houses and Longland Villas, Western Villas and Villas Road have been built *c.*1920s. The large stone house on the extreme left of centre is the former home of the Mountney family, Mr Mountney resided here after he finished as the landlord of the Hurt Arms. (The small building attached on the left is an old nailers' workshop and still exists today.) The large house opposite on the right called West View was the former residence of Bernard Glossop, clerk, surveyor and sanitary inspector to Heage UDC. The Gratton family have lived here for many years. In 1895 the following 'businesses' were recorded in old Toadmoor: Isaac Beighton (cowkeeper, Toad Moor Hill); Louis Machin (cowkeeper); William Blackham: (shopkeeper and wire drawer); Tom Allison Glossop (fire and life insurance agent); Mrs Mary Rostron (greengrocer); Mrs Eliza Watson and Thomas Elliot (property owners).

The author's house is just visible in the central cluster of cottages as Toadmoor Lane winds to the right. Only three houses are visible at this time on Newbridge Road. The right-hand end cottage of the central row off Toadmoor Lane here used to be a smallholding. The farmhouse on the upper right was Toadmoor Farm and is now one of the leading residences in Ambergate and is now named Hillside Cottage.

Arms Hotel built to replace it. 1876 was also the year that Richard Johnson and Nephew (John Thewlis Johnson) opened their new wire works alongside the River Derwent just north of the village. Ambergate was chosen as a most suitable site for a wire manufactory due to the ample water supply of the Derwent and the fact that Ambergate village men were deemed to have the necessary physical strength to enable them to become competent wire drawers.

In 1908 further growth was achieved when James Francis Stevenson opened up his dye works at Bull Bridge, Ambergate, after first establishing the business in Belper in 1893.

Ambergate is everything that Belper is

not, being small with few amenities. The village is really in two parts: that you see on the main Matlock Road (A6) through the village centre; and the now densely populated hillside which Hag Wood once covered.

Ambergate did not have a benefactor such as the philanthropic Strutt family of Belper. However, the wire works of the Johnson family did secure local employment for a period of 120 years, together with supporting and providing for Ambergate's annual Flower & Sports Show which became one of the largest in England. By 1931 the Ambergate population had increased to 901, and over the years many large prestigious houses were built to house works managers and other worthies, many of whom feature in this book.

Ambergate has for over 100 years been a successful and enthusiastic cricketing village, a tradition still enjoyed today. Alas, local employment opportunities with the railway and lime works are now completely lost, although other opportunities have arisen with LB Plastics and J.C.Balls construction and excavation company.

Ambergate is amply served by two main roads and the railway and by 1951 the population had risen to 1,794.

The industry and growth is illustrated in the following pages and many of the images were taken by an unknown photographer who operated *c.*1905-1920 and to whom we must be eternally grateful.

It is the author's hope that this section, being the first of its kind ever published on Ambergate, will be enjoyed by his many local friends acquired over the past 11 years and by others who are interested in the 'Gateway to the Peak'.

The Railway at Ambergate

Ambergate Station: The unique triangular junction has been photographed from the hillside near Hag Wood, high above the former stationmaster's house in the lower foreground looking north. This was Ambergate's third station, built by Messrs W. & H.Harris and opened on 10 December 1876 and had platforms on each side of the double tracks to form an open triangle serving trains coming from Derby to Manchester and to Sheffield and trains coming from Manchester towards the Erewash Valley as well as the local services to Mansfield via the Ambergate and Pye Bridge line. Sprinklings of snow are evident in this 1904 view. Chase Farm (now Johnson's Club) is on the upper left with Chase Cottage on the upper right accessed under the railway and over the hump-back canal bridge.
The message on the reverse is from a W.Steeples of Derwent Terrace, Ambergate, to G.A.Fletcher at Milford, regarding hymn sheets. W.Steeples was a Sunday School officer at the old Wesleyan Chapel on Newbridge Road. Ambergate West Junction signal box stands on the centre Matlock line. Voted 'Mr Ambergate' twice in three years, the popular Mr Philip Smith now owns much of the land to the top right of this picture, close to the woods.

Prior to the formation of the Midland Railway Company in 1844, from three original companies, the route of the then North Midland Railway through Ambergate was considered to be the most difficult line of route. In 1846, Samuel Bagshaw's *Derbyshire Directory* described the route: 'This county now enjoys by its railroads pre-eminent means of facilitating general communications and commercial intercourse. The Derby and Leeds section or North Midland Great Trunk railway, which constitutes a central link between the other important railways in the north, centre and south of England is 72½ miles long with upwards of 200 bridges and seven tunnels, in its course measuring together nearly two and a quarter miles. The cost was about £3,000,000, though the estimate was £1,500,000. The whole line was completed in a little more than three years. George and Robert Stephenson with their assistant, Mr Swanwick, were the engineers. It was opened through all this county and as far as Rotherham on 11 May 1840 and throughout the whole of the line on 1 July 1840.

'From Derby, the North Midland railways run northwards, by Duffield and other villages through Milford Tunnel, 836 yards in length with rich and handsome arched frontings, to Belper through which it runs in a cutting lined with masonry. At this place it has no less than 12 bridges crossing it in the space of a mile. It then crosses (by two timber bridges each almost 400ft in length and containing 200,000 cubic feet of timber) Belper pool, where the Derwent expands in a broad sheet, with a wooded island in the midst. A short tunnel,

Ambergate Station: This is Ambergate's triangular station looking southwards with the Hurt Arms and St Anne's on the right. The long flight of steps up to platforms 2 & 3 are visible in the centre of the triangle. The large stationmaster's house and two greenhouses of Robert Manners, together with the railway cottages, are on the left with Hag Wood behind them. The waiting room on platform 3 was at one time used by the Ambergate Home Guard and was destroyed by fire in the late 1950s.
Ambergate's former second station buildings are visible in the distant right, opposite St Anne's Church, with the covered over Longlands Tunnel beyond the old Ambergate South Junction signal box in the distant right past the arched viaduct. The block of five cottages on the left were built by J.Walker & Sons in 1894 to cater for the increase in railway staff. The rent was 4s per week.

a fine viaduct across the Derwent and another short tunnel at Hag Wood (Toadmoor) are then passed, and the grand and interesting works at the principal crossing of the Derwent are reached. The river runs in the bottom of the valley, with the turnpike road at some distance above it, the railroad passes obliquely over both by a magnificent viaduct, and in the same place, is itself crossed by the Cromford Canal in an aqueduct built by the Company.

'Bull Bridge and Lodge Hill tunnel, 250yds in length, and South Wingfield station are then passed, the column of Crich Stand, where mountain limestone abounds, being seen on the left on the distant hills. After passing a deep and extensive cutting, opened out into the romantic valley of the Amber. . . .'

The Manchester, Buxton, Matlock and Midland Junction Railway: This railway was originally projected to run from the Ambergate Station of the Midland Railway by Matlock to Buxton to the London and North Western Railway near Manchester, length 45 miles and the act for the purpose was obtained on 16 July 1846. The line was, however, only constructed to a distance of 11½ miles from Ambergate to Rowsley. This section was opened on 4 June 1849. The Cromford Canal, 17 miles long, was subsequently purchased by the company by powers conferred by their Act of Incorporation and the Cromford Canal Sale Act of 1846. The price was £101,200 and in 1852 the whole concern, railway and canal, was leased for 19 years to the Midland and LNW Railway Co's jointly at a rent of 2½ per cent per annum. The railway ran from Ambergate in a north-westerly direction up the valley of the River Derwent to Rowsley. In its course it had no less than six tunnels, two of which passed under the celebrated Matlock High Tor. In 1857 there were five passenger trains each way daily and several luggage trains daily.

There is no doubt that prior to the railway passing through it, the hamlet of Toadmoor would not have developed into the village of Ambergate as we know it today.

Ambergate Station: This 1904 photograph was taken on the same day as the view on page 121 with snow on the lower left and in the upper fields. This view provides a good record of the rear yard to the station house and buildings. The old stationmaster's house was demolished and rebuilt on this site about 1847. The buildings on the right were part of the former Thatched House Tavern. Hag Wood is in the right foreground and the lime kilns top right. The large stationmaster's house of Robert Manners on the left has recently been divided up to provide separate dwellings. Ambergate North Junction signal box stands on the extreme right.

Turnbull Hill from the station: The three-carriage steam train has just drawn into the northbound platform 1. The ten fine gable-fronted houses on Turnbull Hill, accessed off Chase Road, are clearly visible in this 1937 view by Lilywhite Ltd. These houses were auctioned off in the Hurt Arms by local entrepreneur and builder, Teddy Glossop.

Midland Railway Station: Twelve Midland Railway servants, including the stationmaster, pose for Kingsway's photographer in this mid-afternoon *c.*1910 view. This scene was taken from the footbridge between platforms 1 and 2/3 looking north. Many enamel advertisements adorn the fencing on platform 1. The large wooden sign states 'Ambergate Junction for Matlock, Rowsley, Bakewell, Buxton and Manchester'. The stationmaster, Robert Manners, is fifth from the left with several porters, a clerk and telegraph clerk included. Henry C.Johnson was the superintendant engineer whilst Mrs Lizzie Clutterbuck was the manageress of the station's refreshment rooms. The building behind is that of the stationmaster's office and parcel office.

The station lost the majority of its main line services on 6 March 1967 and became an unstaffed halt from 1 January 1968. All platforms, with the exception of the Derby to Matlock line, are now lost together with all waiting rooms and buildings. A commuter line from Derby to Matlock still provides a valuable service into the Peak.

Midland Railway: This *c.*1911 view shows the Midland Railway Johnson 4-4-0451 express standing at Ambergate South Junction. The old ornate Dutch gabled building used to form part of Ambergate's second station opened in 1863 and are believed to have been designed by Sir Joseph Paxton. The station remained in use until the new triangular station opened in 1876. The buildings remained *in situ* as the railway superintendent's office and stores until demolished in 1971 after the earlier commissioning of the Derby Power signal box and new colour light signalling scheme. Ambergate's first station, named Amber Gate, was constructed north of Toadmoor tunnel and was in the Jacobean style with Dutch gables and mullioned windows and designed by Francis Thompson. After demolition the stone was used for the second station's buildings.

Ambergate Station: Thomas Davidson, the Fritchley grocer and general provisions merchant, has just arrived at Ambergate Station in his pony and cart. The Midland Railway servant has the task of unloading the many leather bags on to his hand cart on this evidently rainy day in 1906. Note the fine ornate gas lamp on platform 4. Mr Davidson was a staunch supporter of the Society of Friends (the Quakers). The railway cottages on the left were built in 1894.

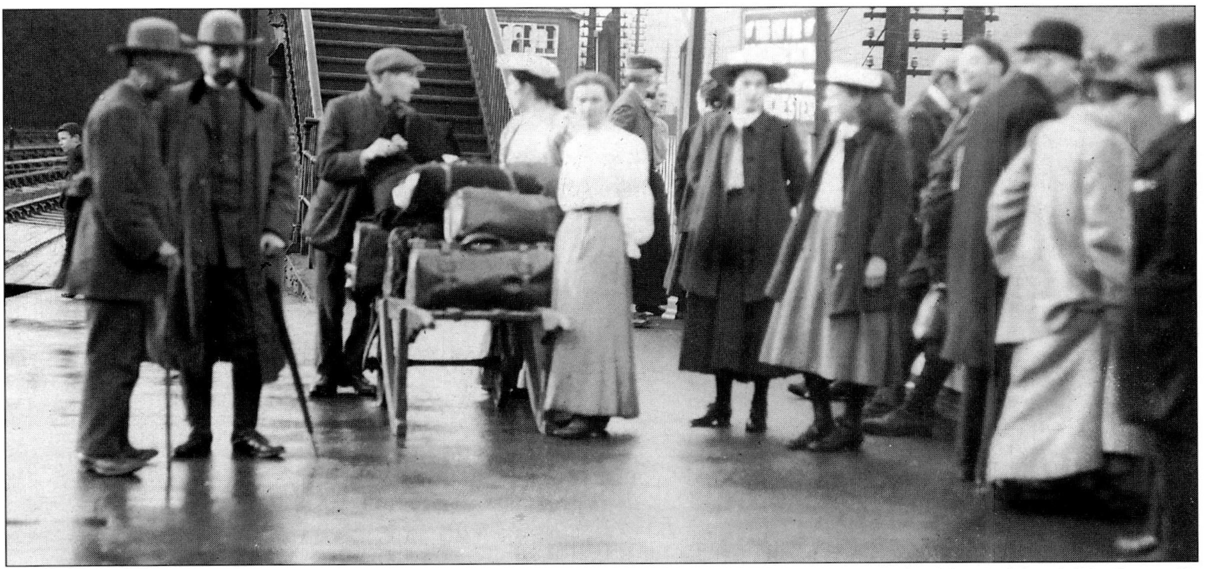

Ambergate Station: In this view Thomas Davidson (with umbrella) is talking to Jesse Darbyshire (with stick), the well-known Fritchley farmer from Barnclose Farm. Many colleagues from the Society of Friends, including Jesse, have turned out to see Mr Davidson off from platform 1 on his long journey to America. Mr Edward Watkins is on the extreme right and he owned the bobbin and moulding/turning factory at Bull Bridge (prior to fire in 1885 it was situated at Fritchley). Ambergate Station signal box is visible to the right of the footbridge steps. The aforementioned two views were part of a specially commissioned set from Harold Burkinshaw, the renowned Belper photographer, to record the beginning of Davidson's journey away from Ambergate. The message on the reverse of the second view, written to Jesse Darbyshire at Barnclose Farm, Fritchley reads: 'Intended bringing the whole of these snaps for you to see, but the wet changed my plans, also Dad went out to tea, so am minding shop. If you're in town and can call at Studios please do – or will try next Sunday. Signed H.B. (Harold Burkinshaw).' The card was posted on 21 October 1906. Davidson visited America in 1906 and 1908 whilst Jesse Darbyshire visited America in 1905.

Ambergate Station: 74 members of the Royal Dublin Fusiliers stand to attention – apart from the officer on the right with his hand in his pocket – on the wooden platform 6 of Ambergate Station. This important and rare view by an unknown local photographer is entitled 'H.Co 2nd RDF, Railway Strike, 1911.' Chase Cottage and outbuildings are behind over the canal bank.

Ambergate Station: This late 1930s view, showing a goods train coming from Derby towards Ambergate station, was taken from under the footbridge between platforms 1 and 2. The old Midland style Ambergate Station's signal box stands on the right. Note the old lower quadrant mechanical semaphore signal has been cleared for the oncoming train.

Toadmoor Tunnel: The Railway Technical Centre, Derby, took this mid-1960s photograph of Toadmoor Tunnel, shown here as Railway Bridge No 44. The tunnel was 128 yds long and cut through an unstable hillside on a notoriously difficult line of route. George Stephenson decided that the tunnel should be constructed in an elliptical shape, so that it had least diameter in the vertical direction and most resistance at, its sides and is also braced with steel hoops at its southern end. The cutting of Hag Wood (later renamed Toadmoor) Tunnel took 15 months instead of the estimated two due to unplanned earth movements.

Ambergate Goods Shed: This late 1930s photograph shows the former Ambergate Goods Shed which now belongs to local firm J.C.Balls plant hire and excavation contractors, as does the home on the right. This house was once part of the old Thatched House Tavern and Commercial Hotel which closed as Ambergate's third station and was commissioned in 1876.

The section of railway line through Ambergate was widened between 1928 to 1932 and necessitated the uncovering of the 101-yard Longland tunnel. The Scottish firm of Shanks & McEwan carried out the work to enable the creation of the four-track cutting. The local Butterley Company provided the ironwork for the new bridge which was placed alongside the original to carry two extra tracks over the River Derwent and the main road (A6). Shanks & McEwan employed private locomotives to haul the Longlands tunnel spoil in wagons to be tipped to widen the embankment which catered for the extra tracks. This picture is of an ancient 0-4-0 square Saddle tank with outside cylinders named *Bonnie Dundee* which had been rebuilt by Andrew Barclay, Sons & Co Ltd in 1896 and was employed in 1928-29 along with *Peterhead,* an 0-6-0 saddle tank, on the rewidening scheme.

Bull Bridge Lime Works: The Butterley Iron Company had extensive lime works at Bull Bridge where about 800 tons of lime and 30,000 tons of stone were used annually in 1857. About 50 men were employed at this time and Mr Peter William Browne was the resident manager. Messrs Curtis & Harvey's gunpowder magazine was also situated at Bull Bridge. The Butterley Co had five lime kilns here in 1895. From 1895 through to the late 1920s, John Pakenham Hamilton was the agent. This extremely rare *c.*1905 scene by an unknown local photographer shows a 20-strong workforce plus three of their hard-working horses. Three of the 'management' team are standing on the right.

Lime Works and Spion Kop: This early view was part of Blount's Real Photo Series and refers to the hillside to the rear of the kilns as the Spion Kop (a name from the Boer War). The steep incline of Stephenson's mineral railway is clearly visible to the left. The lime burners of the view below are missing in this fascinating *c.*1908 scene. The site between the kilns and the railway is littered with many 'wigwam' style stacks of wood. Cliff Quarry, Crich, closed in 1957 and in 1959 the locomotive sheds and various buildings were taken over by the Tramway Museum. The limeworks closed on 2 October 1965 after approximately six million tons of limestone had travelled down Stephensons narrow gauge mineral railway to the Ambergate Lime Works. There was obvious pressure from the restrictions of the Clean Air Act and the closure of Wingfield Manor Colliery. The old railway track was dismantled and utilised on the Talyllyn Railway in North Wales. The kilns were demolished in 1966 to make way for a modern gas processing plant.

Ambergate Lime Kilns: The conical hill at Crich contained caverns of lead bearing ore and also large quantities of limestone of a superior quality, quarried by the Butterley partners Outram & Jessop and later by the railway celebrity George Stephenson. Stephenson leased Cliff Quarry north of the village and he originally constructed eight kilns at Ambergate to the west of Bull Bridge on the line of the railway and laid his own wagon way down the side of the Amber Valley, ending it in what came to be known as 'The Steep', a steep self-acting incline which took loaded wagons down the slope to their discharging bays at the Ambergate kilns. In 1841 the eight kilns were extended to 20 kilns. The curving bank of kilns were each between 30 and 40ft in depth, 11ft in diameter, with cones 20ft high. The stone was brought part of the way from Crich Cliff by locomotive and on two inclined planes worked by wire ropes, one of which was supposed to be the steepest in the kingdom, being 500 yds long and rising 1 in 10. The wagons were let down by a brake attached to a large winding drum. The other incline was 600 yards long rising 1 in 36 and worked by a wire rope round a horizontal shield. There was about one mile of railroad and another inclined plane longer than either of the other two. In 1846, 80 men were employed and aided by a steam engine of 10hp. By 1857, 120 men were employed and the engine increased to 12hp. The sale of lime and stone increased from 40,000 tons in 1846 to between 50,000 and 60,000 tons per annum by 1857. The lime was generally used as an agricultural fertiliser. In 1857 Chas Binns of Clay Cross was the principal agent with Mr Thomas Summerside the resident agent and manager. Mr Robert Boag was the lime burner and contractor with Mr James Jefferies the contractor of the quarries. At night the flames shooting from the 20 cones was a spectacular sight. The pre-heating and mechanised feeding were added to the kilns *c.*1909.

Lime Works Railway: This somewhat faded *c.*1930s amateur photograph of Crich Lime Works Railway, Ambergate, shows a train standing at the engine shed at Chadwick Nick Lane, hauled by the 3ft 3in gauge 0-4-0 tank *Hodder*. The loco was brought from a dealer at Matlock, called Twiggs, and used to be at the Celanese Works at Spondon.

'Limestone Cracker': This extremely rare view shows an old charabanc style motor vehicle on the road from Ripley, having passed over the original stone bridge over the River Amber. In the background stands the substantial Limestone Cracker for breaking large pieces of limestone into small pieces.Apparently the noise was horrendous. Ambergrove is near here along with the Council Depot. It is said that just after World War Two a lady car driver crashed through the bridge into the Amber and when she was pulled out, she was wearing only a fur coat!

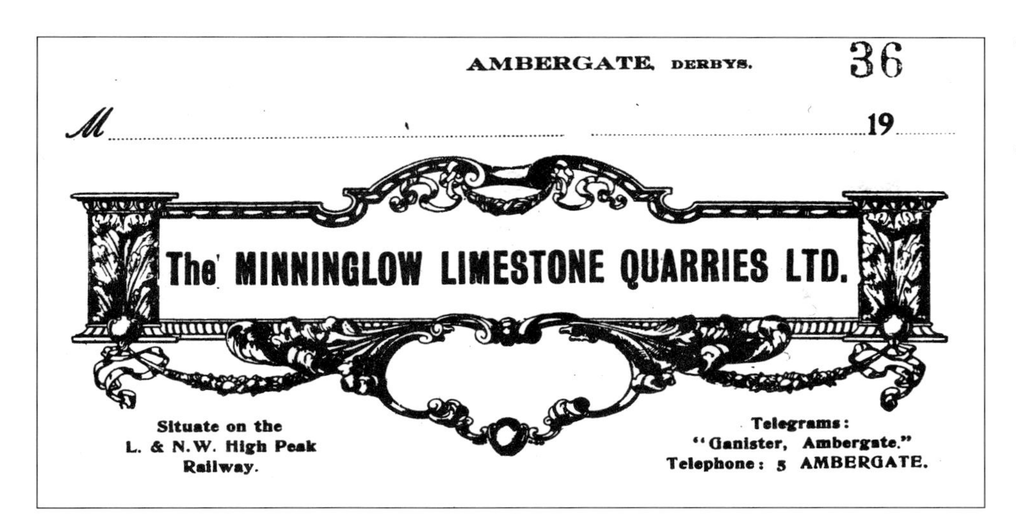
AMBERGATE, DERBYS. 36

M.. ....19..........

The MINNINGLOW LIMESTONE QUARRIES LTD.

Situate on the
L. & N.W. High Peak
Railway.

Telegrams:
"Ganister, Ambergate."
Telephone: 5 AMBERGATE.

This ornate billhead is from The Minninglow Limestone Quarries Ltd of Ambergate. They were situated on the L & NW High Peak Railway.

The Aquaducts and Canal

The Cromford Canal opened in 1794 running from Cromford Wharf, on the site of Arkwright's mills, clinging to the River Derwent for 1¼ miles as far as Leawood where it swung to the east to cross the river by the Wigwell Aqueduct. At Ambergate it turned still further east, crossed the Amber Valley

Bull Bridge: Another rare *c.*1910 scene taken by unknown photographer. On the immediate left stands the Canal Inn (run by John W.Radford in 1912) advertising Hardy's Gold Medal Ales. On the bottom right stands the whitewashed building of the Lord Nelson public house run by Henry Lock who was recorded as the victualler here and also as a farmer. Francis Stevenson & Co's early dye works are situated out of view close to the Lord Nelson. Opposite here the old gasometer and manufactory complete with chimney are visible. These belonged to the Ambergate, Crich, Bull Bridge and Fritchley Gas Light & Coke Co Ltd. The old bobbin and moulding works of Edward Watkin & Co are also nearby. Note the open fields where Stevenson's present-day factory shop and car park now stand. The plant for loading the stone dominates the left side of the canal, with several Midland Railway wagons in view. This view was taken from the vicinity of Hag Lane and in the upper right is the hamlet of Saw Mills which had its origins in the stone and marble works formerly carried out here. The chimney of the old brick works (later General Refactories) is on the extreme right. Graves Wood is on the top right. The path of the old canal can be traced on its journey from one side of the Ripley Road to the other.

by a second aqueduct, this time at Bull Bridge, and on to Butterley Ironworks by means of a 3,000-yard tunnel descended by a series of 14 locks to meet the Erewash Canal at Langley Mill. William Jessop constructed the Bull Bridge Aqueduct which carried the canal over the River Amber and the Ripley Road (A610) on a high embankment 200 yds long. This was demolished in 1968 to permit road widening. Wigwell Aquaduct still stands and was also built by Jessop. In its heyday the canal carried coal, coke, gritstone, iron-ore, lead and limestone from Crich to serve as flux in the Butterley furnaces. The canal was sold to the railway in 1852 and by 1889 the traffic was only local. The upper part to Cromford was closed by the LMS Railway in 1944. The British Waterways Board took it over but by 1974 ownership passed to Derbyshire County Council. Only the portion between Cromford and Wigwell Aqueduct is open, thanks to the aid of the Cromford Canal Society. The Ambergate portion of the canal frequently froze over in the winter and skating became a popular weekend amusement.

Bull Bridge: Bull Bridge in 1895 was described as being a busy little village on the bank of the River Amber 1¼ miles south-east of Crich. As well as the Butterley lime works and Stevenson's dye works, the bobbin and moulding works of Edward Watkins & Co were situated here after their removal from Fritchley in 1885. This *c.*1940s locally-produced photograph is taken from just past the railway bridge looking up towards Crich. The Lord Nelson stands on the left, and the entrance to Stevenson's car park and old gas works is on the right. This turn, now called Drovers Way, was at one time named Gas Lane. The small building on the corner was once part of the gas offices. On the right, out of view, an old flour mill stood where Stevenson's lower car park exists.

Stevenson's Dye Works

The start of the Stevenson's family business was in the period of the great Industrial Revolution. In 1825, James Stephenson (note surname spelling) started to bleach cotton tape in a mill powered by water near Wirksworth. He later changed his name to Stevenson and in 1850 a steam engine was installed to replace the water wheel and the business began to prosper. In 1865 James' youngest son, James Henry, opened the family's first dyeing department near to his father's mill. He dyed the bleached cotton tape and silk and cotton yarns. The dyeing vessels were crude, being made of hollowed out tree trunks called 'barks'. The tape and yarns were suspended across the barks on long wooden poles, and were turned by a man standing at each end. The dyes used were natural products such as cochineal (bright red and extracted from beetles) and logwood (black and made by grinding up tree bark). These dyes were used in conjunction with metals (in the form of salts), such as lead, iron, copper and tin, to change the shades and to improve dye fastness. As the business grew it moved to Duffield where the mill was better sited.

The company further expanded to Derby in 1874 but fell into difficulties when their main customer, Tatlow's of Wirksworth, closed in 1877, and James Henry died in 1878 at the age of 76. In 1893, James Francis Stevenson, James Henry's son, established his dye works in the High Street, Belper and eventually opened a shop at 80 King Street. The works at Bull Bridge, Ambergate, were established in *c.*1908-10. In 1912 Frank (Francis) lived in Derby Road, Belper, before moving to 26 Albert Street, Belper.

James Francis died in 1957 and his son, A.Francis Malcolm Stevenson, became chairman. The firm merged with the Nottingham Manufacturing Co in 1963 and ceased to be a family-run business. Malcolm resigned in 1966, servering all Stevenson links. He died in 1995.

The firm has offered local employment for over 100 years and is now called Stevenson's Fashion Dyers and currently employs 628 people and is now part of the Coates Vyella Group. In 1970, incidentally, there were 1,400 employees.

F.Stevenson & Co's Amber Dye Works: This is one of the earliest known photographs of the original dye works at Bull Bridge, *c.*1912. James Francis Stevenson purchased the site from the Strutt family, moving here in the early 1900s. The business thrived and new buildings were added in 1910.

The Ironing Shed: These rare early interior scenes (*above and below*) show the women carrying out their hand ironing duties at Stevenson's. Note the low lying wicker trays so as to avoid getting the garments dirty on the floor. The exact dates are unknown but are believed to be *c.*1907 when much of the work was carried out in old huts and makeshift buildings. Note the three old steam presses in the bottom picture. Both are interior views of the building pictured on the previous page.

Checking and Bagging: This is the start of the process where up to 17 local women are checking the tubes of nylon from customers such as Ariston, Wolsey, Co-op, Brettles and Blounts. They counted out into lots and put into the square container trolleys.

Shaping Process: The next step is to place the nylon hose over the wooden leg shapes, termed pre-boarding, before dying where they pass through the Paramould machine in a steam shaping process. They are then arranged into batches of two dozen. The man holding the wooden leg (extreme right) is George Curzon.

Dyeing Process: The next stage is to place the bags of hose into the dyeing machines. The various recipes for colour and shades are placed on the machines. The final process (not shown) after dyeing is to place items in a trolley and forward to the Schusters machine where hose is again placed on shaping boards, seams added and tops straightened before entering the heat chamber to set them. The Schusters machines were very long and usually employed three people at each end.

King Street: This pre-World War One photograph shows a young Miss Kathleen Ivy (the daughter of James Francis) in the shop doorway of Frank Stevenson & Co on King Street, Belper. They were dyers and specialists in dry cleaning, with other branches at Matlock, Ripley, Mansfield, Lincoln and Newark. On both sides of the doorway the windows are neatly laid out with ribbons and flowers. The right-hand window appears to advertise the cleaning of fur stoles. The premises were adjacent to Albert James Cash, solicitor, and both Cash & Stevenson's were listed as being in the premises situated at 80 King Street. This site is still double-fronted and was Edna Clamp's confectioners after Stevenson's but is now a popular book shop run by Maggie Hull. James F.Stevenson and Miss C.G.Stevenson (perhaps his daughter) lived at 26 Albert Street, Belper, now called The Laurels (see page 100). Alderman A.J.Cash, who was also a foundation governor at Herbert Strutt's

Stevenson family: Mr Frank Stevenson is believed to be in this group photograph by Frederick Holbrook of George Street in what was a specially-commissioned turn-of-the-century picture. The ladies all wear high-collared dresses and all are in their Sunday best. Many of the Stevenson family, along with some of their workers, are featured here.

The Keeper's Cottage: This is an extremely rare sepia photograph showing a private contractor's engine and five wagons on the narrow Derwent Valley Water Board railway line. This line was to enable the construction of their underground reservoir near to Crich. Work began in June 1907 and was completed by July 1911. Water was brought from Bamford by an aqueduct. Two railways were on site, one to bring stone from a nearby quarry and one to take away spoil. One line was worked by an Orenstein-Koppel 0-4-0 well tank locomotive (seen above Keeper's Cottage). An old lady stands by a crudely constructed gate to her old stone cottage which was situated in the area known as Bowmer Rough. The term Keeper's Cottage probably stems from the keeper of the forest in Chase Woods. Sadly only a few remnants exist of this cottage today.

Contractors' Engine: This somewhat faded, originally sepia, photograph shows contractors in an unknown location with their horses and cart. Behind stands the contractors' 2ft gauge engine No.1480 named *Sydney* built in Berlin in 1905 by Orenstein & Koppel. The message on the reverse side refers to Messrs Hawkville & Wright working on the building of Ambergate Waterworks and Reservoir in 1910.

Derwent Valley Water Board way from reservoir: This *c.*1910, originally sepia, photograph features the unusual narrow gauge elevated inclined wagonway utilised by the Derwent Valley Water Board. The scene accurately pinpoints the location of this intricate construction just a few feet away from the stone cottages (left) situated on the Ripley Road (A610). Many thousands of pipes had to be laid to provide water from the Crich hillside into the reservoir near Belper. On the right stands the goods shed and the station buildings which were once part of the 'Thatched House Tavern' Hotel.

Ambergate Wire Works and The Johnson Family

John Thewlis Johnson, the grandson of John Johnson, was born in 1836 and first began work within his family firm in 1860. In 1865 he formed a partnership with his uncle, Richard Johnson, following John's death in 1863. Hence the Manchester firm was called Richard Johnson & Nephew. The Johnsons relied heavily on the skills of master wire drawer George Bedson, and together they were involved in supplying wire for the cross-Channel telegraph. In 1872 both Thewlis and Bedson travelled to Ambergate with a view to expanding their business. Thewlis bought an old nail industry forge. After the installation of water turbines and plant, the Ambergate Wire Works were officially opened on 22 May 1876. T.D.Crozier, employed at the Manchester works, became the first wire works manager at Ambergate and he was with R.J.& N. for 45 years until his death in 1884. The firm quickly gained a reputation for the production of superior wire. Thewlis took a personal interest in the welfare of his employees who respected him as a fair employer, and his motto was 'Virtus Patientia Veritas'. Thewlis' first son called Herbert (Bertie) was born in 1866 and his second son, Ernest, in 1870. It was during 1870 that the Johnsons enhanced their credibility by supplying wire for the West Indies and Panama Cable and the China, Singapore and Carpentoria Cable. Thewlis died in 1895 at the age of 59 following pneumonia, having been a partner in the firm for more than 30 years. As the sole owner he bequeathed the wire works to his two sons, Bertie (29) and Ernest (25).

Richard Johnson
1809-1881

John Thewlis Johnson
1836-1896

A Mr Joseph Briggs came to Ambergate in 1873 to work as a goods porter on the Midland Railway. In 1875 he began work at Johnson's wire works and by 1883 he succeeded in becoming the works manager, a post he held until 1910. He retired to his home at Mossley Villas to indulge in his hobby of repairing violins, and was succeeded by Arthur Kay in 1910. He had been at Ambergate for 30 years. Both sons rose through the ranks after war broke out: Colonel Herbert Johnson commanded the 17th Manchester Regiment; Ernest joined the Duke of Lancaster's Yeomanry and became a major.

In 1919, after returning from the war where Herbert sustained a severe leg wound at the Battle of the Somme, a celebration was arranged in Ambergate in November 1919 as a victory and sports celebration. The Ambergate works became Bertie's responsibility and generally hard steel was drawn. He was admired by wire drawers who referred to him as 'the Colonel'. There was always a staff excursion and in 1889 it took the form of a cricket match at Baslow where the Bradford XI defeated Ambergate by 46 runs to 28. In 1900 it was to the Dukeries. After each excursion lunch, a senior member of staff would always propose this toast to the firm:

Colonel Herbert Johnson
1866-1923

> "May the present heads enjoy good health which is more valuable than riches.
> "May they always have plenty of orders at good prices and plenty of rods to execute the same.
> "May their galvanising baths never leak or their rolling mills break down.
> "May they never have any bad debts and now stand to your glasses and drink properly to the firm."

The outing in 1920 was to the Colonel's home at Allestree Hall. The Colonel's former home was

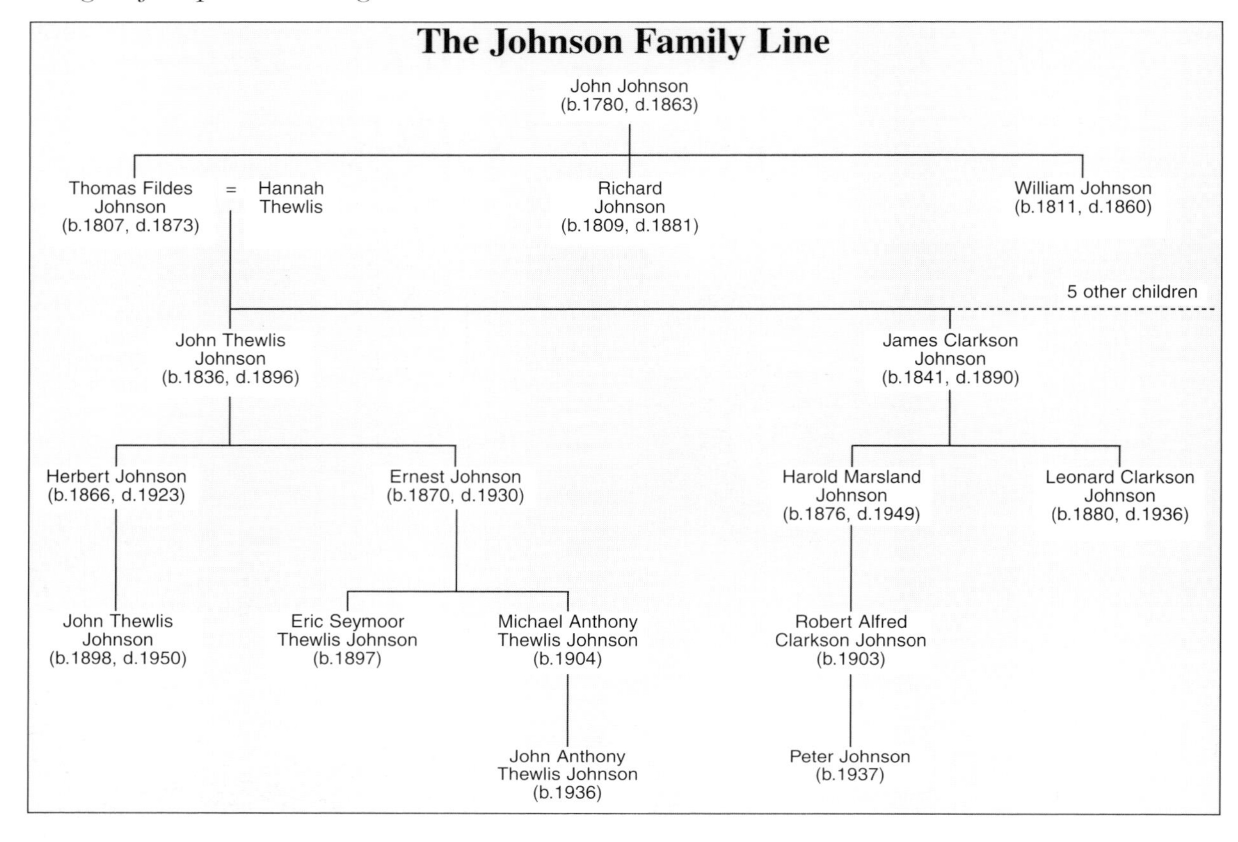

Farnah Hall, moving to Allestree in 1916. He was a church warden at St Edmund's Allestree and a representative of the Diocesan Council. (the Johnsons had a benevolent fund for their workers where ancilliary workers paid 1d per week which was matched by the Johnsons.) During the war years the Johnsons concentrated on war priority items but by 1921 trade was very depressed due to continental manufacturers (protected tariff walls). Such post-war problems led to many of Johnson's wire drawers being laid off for up to six months. The Colonel did his best to see that staff were not discharged. Walter Wragg and Frank Wood worked many years for the firm as did Arthur Holmes, whose father had been head gardener at Oakhurst. The hours were often long, 6.30am to 4.30pm being normal both in summer and winter. Apprentices took five years to learn their trade and their 'box', given to them by the firm and containing a dozen punches, setting hammer and a pair of pulling pliers, became one of their most prized possessions.

Sadly Bertie died on 7 July 1923 and the wire works closed for a day with many employees attending his funeral. The Colonel's widow (Ethel Alexandra Bernard) died in 1928 and Allestree Hall's contents were put up for sale.

Michael Johnson (Ernest's son) entered the Manchester side of the family firm in 1925. Richard Johnson & Nephew became a public company in 1928 with Ernest Johnson as chairman, but he died of pneumonia in early 1930. Sir Walter Campbell was appointed as chairman, the first time a Johnson had not headed the firm for 167 years. Mr F.A.Stackpole became general manager, quickly replaced by Mr D.H.Sawtell. The firm's lowest-ever recorded tonnage was in 1931 when both Manchester and Ambergate works produced only 30,000 tons of steel wire. In the autumn there was a serious flood at Ambergate which hindered their progress with 3ft of water from the Derwent rushing through the works. It was Robert Johnson who managed the firm's difficulties. Michael Johnson succeeded Sir Walter Campbell in 1936, as chairman, and by 1937 net profits had increased by 56per cent. However, during the first four years as a public company the Ambergate works had incurred losses. In 1938 Ian Fairholme came to Ambergate and Robert Johnson became a director and he made it his business to know all his workforce by their first names. W.H.Rogerson became sales director after starting life at Johnson's as an office boy. During 1940 both Michael and Robert Johnson served in the Local Defence Volunteers (Home Guard), and at Ambergate, Ian Fairholme commanded the Volunteers. Through out the war years Ambergate was in full production. However, in 1943 an electrical fault caused a serious fire necessitating the temporary transfer of the Ambergate workers to Manchester. During 1947 a fuel crisis closed the Ambergate works for two weeks. Ian Fairholme was elected to the board in 1957 and retired in 1970. Philip Rambout succeeded Michael Johnson upon his retirement in 1969 with Oliver Jessel taking the chair by 1972.

Johnson's male voice choir, founded in 1914, was very popular and gave local concerts. In fine weather the choir would take an hour for their dinner break and go into the woods at the back of the works to practice.

The following products were once household names: Johnsons Resistee, Johnsons Wire Bulwork, Johnsons Shorthorn Barb Wire, Johnsons Dreadnought Wire, Johnsons Special Hornet Barb Wire and Johnsons First Class Galvanizing.

Alas, the present firm of Bridon Ropes which now owns Richard Johnson & Nephew, appear to be in the throes of closure and Ambergate may lose a source of employment that has been part of the village for nearly 120 years.

The Wire Works: Lilywhite Ltd produced this late 1920s view of the Wire Works, Ambergate. In 1895 Bulmer described the works: 'About ½ mile above Halfpenny Bridge which spans the Derwent are the wire mills of Messrs Richard Johnson & Nephew, established in 1876 as a branch of their forges and wiremills in Manchester. The works comprise a large block of stone buildings, which stretch upwards of 300 yards along the bank of the river, and are driven by two turbines, probably the largest in England. About 250 workmen are employed here. The firm has been in existence upwards of a century. Near the works are the ruins of a blast furnace erected in 1764 for the manufacture of iron for nails and sheets. Charcoal was exclusively used, and the ore was brought by packhorses. The works were often referred to as the Alderwasley Works.'
The old weir is evident on the left. The large stone house on the right was the home of the various works managers and Ian Fairholme once resided here prior to its demolition after World War Two. The chimney belongs to the boiler house, whilst the long building is where wire was drawn on the second floor. The main drawing mill is situated to the rear.

Wire Works: This pre-World War One Kingsway Series illustration, showing the old weir and lattice bridge, has the wire works warehouse on the left. The house on the right after passing over the lattice work bridge was at one time home to Bill Fern and family, night-watchman. It later became an ambulance and rest room.

The Wire Works: Our unknown local photographer has again captured an interesting view of the wire works, Oakhurst is clearly in view on the left. Situated opposite the works on the other side of the main Matlock Road, Johnson's had their own private sidings and signal box. All their raw materials were once brought in and finished goods dispatched by rail from the station. Originally the goods were taken to the railway sidings by horse-drawn carts. The large chimney in the centre acted as a flue for fumes and Jim Wooley used to clean it once a year by hand. This scene gives a clear view of the wire cleaning sheds where acids were employed. Shining Cliff Woods are in the background.

Donkey cart: The well-kept donkey and cart belong to Mrs Johnson of Oakhurst. The simple message penned to the reverse side of this card reads: 'Mrs Johnson, Ambergate, Derbyshire.' This view is believed to be taken near the former Oakhurst stables. The donkey used to be kept in the orchard.

Johnson's lorry: This scarce photograph shows a brand-new Foden lorry built for Richard Johnson & Nephew Ltd, the wire manufacturers. ONU 471 is standing outside the gates of the Foden factory where it was built.

Oakhurst

In 1895 the following reference was recorded: 'Oakhurst, a commodious mansion, was erected in 1848, by Francis Hurt and enlarged in 1888 and 1894. It occupies an elevated situation on the right bank of the River Derwent and is surrounded by a small park.

'The house is illuminated throughout by the electric light. The dynamo is driven by a small turbine worked by water supplied from a reservoir in the wood hard by. Near an old disused quarry, is a cave which was used as a blacksmith's shop when millstones were quarried here, before the introduction of French stones.'

John Thewlis Johnson purchased Oakhurst from Francis Edward Hurt *c.*1872 just about the period when he first purchased the old nailmakers forge, whilst his partner and uncle, Richard Johnson, leased Alderwasley Hall from Francis Edward Hurt from 1876-1880, Thewlis Johnson lived at Oakhurst until his death in 1895, and during his time here he employed a butler, a footman, maids and a host of gardeners and grooms. The Oakhurst gardens were cared for by the very capable head gardener George Holmes, who had previously worked for the Duke of Devonshire at Chatsworth. George Holmes was the prime mover in the formation of Ambergate Cricket Club and was involved as secretary-treasurer, captain, vice-captain, groundsman, chairman and president at one time or another before his death in 1941.

In 1912, Thewlis' widow who still lived in Oakhurst gave a magnificent supper at the Public Hall, Belper, to commemorate the wedding of her son Gerald Johnson. More than 500 men and their wives attended. Every man was given a packet of tobacco and each lady a box of chocolates.

Oakhurst: Lilywhite Ltd of Sowerby Bridge produced this view in *c.*1929 of the former Johnson family home, Oakhurst. The Johnson family were no longer resident here and Oakhurst had become the Diocesan Retreat House. It was dedicated by the Bishop of Southwell on Friday 7 November 1924. In 1928, Sister Mary was recorded as the deaconess here. The huge lean-to greenhouse, formerly tended by head gardener George Holmes, is on the left. The three-storey left-hand portion of the house with the ornate black and white curved timbers and arched upper window was added in 1888 by the Johnsons. The Diocesan connection remained into the early 1940s until the Army took it over as a HQ under the control of Colonel Hamilton. Jimmy Bell. Margaret Murphy, signal teleprinter operator for the ATS, was also in service here. After the war Oakhurst was divided up into nine flats, in 1947, and these remained into the mid-1970s until several occupants were offered council homes by Heage UDC. Oakhurst then began its spiral of deterioration.

Oakhurst: In Bulmer's 1895 *Directory* both John Thewlis Johnson and his son Herbert were recorded at Oakhurst, as was their bailiff Mr George Fern. It is hard to believe that this once magnificent mansion of the Johnson family now lies derelict and heavily vandalised awaiting demolition. It is hoped, if demolition takes place, that the ornate stone carvings and Hurt/Johnson family crests will be saved. This late 1920s view shows the end and front elevations of Oakhurst.

Francis Scarratt, whose business was then in Derby Market Hall, took this photograph of Oakhurst in 1930. The portion containing the chapel was built in 1894 by the Johnson family approximately one year prior to John Thewlis Johnson's death.

Ambergate multi-view: This 1932 Lilywhite publication shows Oakhurst, St Anne's, Matlock Road, Halfpenny Bridge, and Turnbull Hill. The top left view of Oakhurst shows the original arched entrance which has the inscription 'F.H.' (Francis Hurt) 1848 (the original construction date) over the door.

The original stone arched entrance of Oakhurst, showing the inscription 'F.H' together with the date of construction.

Another stone engraving marking the Johnsons' extension of 1894.

The Chase: This rare view by our local unknown photographer was sent to Willis Glossop Esq., of Albert Villa, Newbold, Chesterfield in September 1904. This is Chase Farm often referred to as Wilmot's Farm after the 1888 owner Robert Hay Wilmot. The building on the left was the cowsheds with the barn to the right. This view is from the rear looking towards the canal with Thomas Summerside's old home visible behind, situated off the canal bank. Much of this charming farm still exists today in the form of Richard Johnson & Nephew's sports club. The old barn now forms the entrance to the new club house, whilst the farmhouse is now the club steward's residence and stores.

Chase Bridge: This is a 1907 coloured publication from the royal publishers of Raphael Tuck & Sons 'Picturesque Counties' Oilette series featuring Derbyshire. This bridge is still *in situ* today, accessed via Chase Road, off the Matlock Road under Bridge No.6 of the former Midland Railway leading to the Cromford Canal and today's nature reserve. Tuck describes it as follows: 'Chase Bridge is a substantial one-arched structure rendered picturesque by the hand of Time and the artistic growth of ivy.'

The Canal: A tranquil scene alongside the Cromford Canal *c.*1907 has been captured by an unknown local photographer. On the left is Hay's Wharf and the irregular stone cottages belonged at this time to Johnson's wire works. The bearded gentlemen, possibly a wire drawer, is trying his luck with rod and reel watched by the three Edwardian children. These cottages today form part of the St John's Adventure Centre. It is at this point that the canal became wider to enable the barges to turn.

Hag Tunnel: This 1906 photograph by an unknown local photographer shows 'Lewis' and 'Percy' on the canal bank at Ambergate and the view is described as being taken on Good Friday. The view shows Hag Tunnel near Bull Bridge. The Ambergate lime kilns were beyond this tunnel. The tunnel has now been filled in along with the canal. It was this stretch of the canal where local wire worker Jimmy Bell tested the depth on his bike after a good lunchtime session! Also, the well-known one-armed postman 'Jack' ended up in the canal at this point, complete with his bike and mail.

A Little Fresh 'Air from Ambergate: This *c.*1910 humorous card, featuring a 'Toby jug' style head with grass growing from it, was published by Wildt & Kray, the famous greeting card publishers of London, and is worth including for the message printed on the back: 'Dear Kate, I hear you have been on the look out for a young man in the Ambergate area. I am at your command and hoping you will send me your photo in return for mine. I am not handsome I admit but nevertheless I am a hard working man and I am sure we should work well together. I am a farmer by trade and I can soon teach you dairy work and how to churn; hoping you will answer my letters. Yours truly.' A similar card exists for Derby and one assumes that this company produced them for towns and villages throughout the country.

St Annes Parish Church, Ambergate: A church dedicated to St Anne was erected here in 1891-92 at a cost of about £1,800, chiefly defrayed by wire manufacturer John Thewlis Johnson Esq of Oakhurst. The church was referred to as a mission church which was dedicated by the Bishop of Southwell and named St Anne's as a compliment to Thewlis's second wife. The church topping-out ceremony was in 1892. It is a handsome edifice of dressed stone in the Early English style comprising epsidal chancel, north and south transepts, nave and north porch. The west gable carries a small bell turret. All the stone was obtained from nearby Ridgeway Quarry and the work reflects great credit on Mr J.Glossop, the builder. Under the church in the basement is a well-lighted Sunday School room attended in *c.*1895 by about 100 children. This unusual view of the church, looking north, was produced by the Valentine Publishing Company.

St Anne's Church: This Valentine Series view *c.*1905 shows the empty fields to the south (prior to Day's Tea Rooms and Promenade Garage) and the second church entrance off Holly Lane is evident. Several plays were held in the basement schoolroom during the early 1890s and were supported by the Johnson family. The tradition is carried on today with the annual pantomine event put on by the Ambergate Players, a lively bunch from all walks of life. Bertie Johnson of the wire works continued the tradition of his father, Thewlis, in providing strawberry teas to the Ambergate choir during the summer.

St Anne's Church: Showing the ornate designs around the chancel arch. The iron pulpit to the left was later removed to the mission church at Sawmills.

St Anne's Church interior: Bulmer's 1895 *Directory* described the interior as the following: 'The chancel arch is pointed and lofty and crossed by a temporary wooden screen surmounted by large cross. The nave is spacious and fitted with open low backed seats. The north transept is used as a choir vestry and the opposite one is intended for an organ chamber. The five windows of the chancel are single lights, those on the north and south sides of the nave are of two lights; and the west window is a large one of three lights given by the Sunday School children. The interior was chastely decorated in 1894 and a new organ by Messrs Young & Son, Manchester, placed in the organ chamber.' The Revd J.E.Colyer was the curate in charge. The register dates from the year 1899 and there are 200 sittings. This *c.*1930s view was published by Raphael Tuck & Sons Ltd and clearly shows that the chancel screen is far from temporary being a fine new addition after World War One. New style gaslamps have also been fitted.

Easter Cards: This Easter card was issued by St Anne's Church, Ambergate. The Easter Dawn shows Angels with the message: 'He shall give his angels charge over thee. Angels to becken me, nearer, my God, to Thee, nearer to thee'. The reverse side advertises the Good Friday and Easter Day services. Harry Eardley Field was the vicar at the time, of the issue of these cards just prior to World War One.

EASTER DAWN.

"He shall give His angels charge over thee." Ps. xci. 11.
"Angels to beckon me, Nearer, my God, to Thee, Nearer to Thee."

St. Anne's, Ambergate.

CHRIST IS RISEN!

"We praise Thee. We bless Thee. We glorify Thee. We give thanks to Thee for Thy great glory."

St. Anne's, Ambergate.

EASTER CARD.

GOOD FRIDAY SERVICES.

Matins	10.15
Three Hours' Service	12 to 3
Evening Prayer and Address ...	6.30

EASTER DAY.

Holy Communion...	7, 8 and (fully Choral) at 11
Evensong	6.3

With best wishes for a Happy and Blessed Easter.

H. E. FIELD, *Vicar.*

Close up view of St Anne's Church, the parish church of Ambergate.

Halfpenny Gate Toll House: The old Halfpenny Gate Toll House, former residence of Joe Wain, was unnecessarily demolished by Bowmer & Kirkland in 1964 after being declared unfit for human habitation. However, with a little resolve it could surely have been refurbished and preserved. It was allegedly called Ferry House, so-called because a ferry was said to have operated across the River Derwent at this point. In this view two local boys can be seen posing for the photographer on the Halfpenny Bridge.

Halfpenny Toll Bridge: This *c.*1905 scene was taken from the footpath leading to Shining Cliff Woods, and looking across to Halfpenny Gate Toll House and St Anne's Church. In 1895 Charles Pratt was the toll collector.

Halfpenny Bridge: This superb photograph, taken by George Smith of Crich, clearly shows the construction of the bridge of two spans crossing the River Derwent. This stone bridge was erected in 1792 in place of one that collapsed immediately aft its erection. It was the property of Mr Francis Hurt, Lord of th Manor, and a halfpenny toll was extracted from each passeng

ence its name 'Ha'Penny' Bridge. Prior to the bridge being
uilt a ford existed here and pack horses used to bring coal from
enby Pit over the ford to Ashbourne.

This early 1920s view taken from Halfpenny Bridge published by Blounts shows Woodbine Cottage, later called Holly Dene, on the right with the arched railway bridge over the river and road in the distance. Ambergate South Junction signal box stands on the left. Both Holly Dene and the Halfpenny Bridge Toll House were without electricity and had to draw their water from a well tap just below the old chapel on Newbridge Road.

Holly Dene: Lilywhite Ltd published this mid-1920s view of Holly Dene Cottage situated off Holly Lane over Halfpenny Bridge. This desirable cottage has since received much refurbishment, now has dormer windows in the roof and is now called Trilithon Lodge. It was the one time residence of the Wain family.

Holly Dene: This view of Holly Dene was taken from the opposite river bank looking north towards Halfpenny Bridge. The publisher has quaintly titled the view as Ambergate Dale. The cottage was at one time referred to as Woodbine Cottage and J.H.Hilton, clerk to the wire works, was recorded as living here in 1895.

Sands and Point: Although this photograph by Lilywhite Ltd of Halifax portrays very little, it does record the local name of Sands and Point on the river looking south. Crowds of locals and people from Belper and surrounds used to come here to swim and for picnics. The sand was said to be excellent and with seaside holidays being expensive, here was a handy second option, near Halfpenny Bridge.

The Woods: F.Frith & Co Ltd of Reigate published this sepia postcard titled 'Ambergate Woods entrance' *c.*1920. The view is from the path leading to Shining Cliff Woods with Halfpenny Bridge to the left and Holly Lane to the right. Many years later a small wooden 'shop' stood near here selling sweets and newspapers etc. on a weekend only. Mrs Jackson owned the shop, along with another on Newbridge Road, and was often seen delivering goods at late hours, dressed in her nightie and macintosh.

This view was taken from Ambergate Woods by Frank Scarratt, of Abbey Street, Derby, *c.*1905, looking towards the triangular station. The rooftops in the lower left are those of the former foresters' and keepers' cottages belonging originally to Francis Hurt, Lord of the Manor. At some later date they were purchased by Johnson's wire works.

Mountain Side: This mid-1930s view is of Mountain Side in the woods. This grand house at one time belonged to George Holmes, the Johnsons' head gardener at Oakhurst. The message on the reverse reads: 'Ambergate, 13 August 1937. This gives a good idea of the hilltops, they are lovely.' John Foulkes also lived here after Holmes and he kept cows, selling milk round the village of Ambergate. A first rate nursery selling flowering plants and vegetables was here for many years.

The Wood: This view shows several Edwardian cyclists picnicking around the large tree below the former Hurt keepers' cottages and was part of the Valentine Series published *c.*1904-05.

Betty Kenny's Tree: Not too far from Oakhurst in Shining Cliff Woods on a commanding eminence stood a famous yew tree. In 1895 the following was recorded: '... whose spreading branches, though damaged a few years ago by fire, still ove[r] one another and touch the ground. In a cone shaped hut un[der] this leafy canopy lived Luke and Kate Kenny, charcoal burn[ers]

re they brought up a family of eight children, without ever ·ing entered a house except for the purchase of necessaries.' : portraits of the couple, Luke, at the age of 96, and Kate, 88, were painted by James Wood RA in 1813. These paintings were placed in the drawing room at Alderwasley Hall. It would appear that Kate's name became corrupted to Betty.

Becky Kenny's Tree: This 1920s Blount's Real Photo example shows a man complete with plus-fours, short jacket and a hat not dissimilar to a bowler. The tree appears to be somewhat dead in places but is still very large. In the original caption the name has been corrupted (or misspelt) as Becky, and the statement in the title as being near Crich is misleading.

The Volunteers: This rare photograph was taken by an unknown local photographer in 1910. The interesting message on the reverse side from 'Marie of West Bank', reads: 'My dear M, I thought you might like this P.C. of the Volunteers at Ambergate facing Elliot's shop. They came one weekend and they were a noisy lot'. The postcard was sent to Miss M.Wilson at Bolton Hall, Leyburn, Yorkshire, on 6 September 1910.

The Volunteers are out in force and number over 500 and are mustering in the open field where Dean Road now exists. Over 200 local Ambergate inhabitants have turned out to view the spectacle. Outside the centre cottages stands the horse-drawn Red Cross wagon. The ornate bay-windowed brick built terraced houses on the far left which includes the former grocer's shop of Robert Joel Elliot (later John Thomas Elliot) still look good today, with Elliot's shop now reverting to a private residence. On the near right the rear view of Rose Cottages can be seen. On the opposite side set back stands the former Elliot residence built by Glossops, called 'Riverside'.

The Volunteers: The Volunteers have now made camp and somehow have to fit into the 77 tents that have been pitched. Most of the Ambergate inhabitants are still watching this unusual event. The Vicarage and the start of Eden Bank can be seen on the left, whilst the former United Methodist Free Church can be seen on the opposite side of the main road next to Elliot's grocer's shop.

The church was also known as the Bethel Chapel and is a neat stone edifice with pretty porch and attractive frontage erected in 1869. On the east wall inside there was a handsome marble tablet to the memory of Thomas Summerside, who died in 1880, through whose exertions chiefly this chapel was built. He was a Northumbrian and life-long acquaintance of the celebrated George Stephenson. Both worked for the Clay Cross Co associated with the lime kilns.He published his recollections of the great engineer in 1878. Another monument commemorated William Forwood, who died in 1888. Under the chapel there was a well lighted schoolroom. The chapel later became a private house, and the whereabouts of these valuable memorials are unknown.

Riverside House: The fine double-fronted, detached house set well back from the main Matlock Road close to the river is 'Riverside', the former long-time residence of the Elliots (grocer's). Mr Elliot is believed to be on the left through the trellis archway. Thity-eight people have turned out for this fund-raising occasion during the time of World War One. Many are dressed as pierrots and the placard on the front row says: 'Remember our wounded at the front . . .Our Day'. The message scribbled on the reverse side says: 'Mother (second from right, back row). At Riverside near Post Office, Ambergate'. The message must have been placed many years later, as the third post office was not built until long after this scene.

Hurt Arms Hotel: This magnificent three-storey stone building was erected in 1876 by Francis Hurt as a family and commercial hotel and posting house situated at the junction of the Matlock and Ripley roads. The Hurt Arms replaced the old Thatched House Tavern, a former first-rate commercial, posting and boarding hotel situated close to the railway station where post-horses, flys etc were in readiness at five minutes' notice from the long-time proprietor Mr Benjamin Broadhurst. Mr Winfield Alton was the long-serving landlord of the Hurt Arms, recorded here in 1888 and 1912. Richard Woodhouse was the landlord in the late 1920s-1930s.

The slated porch and large bracket lamp at the entrance were lost many years ago. This clear view was taken by an unknown local photographer from the railway embankment *c.*1912. The stables, built to the same high standard as the hotel, stand to the right-hand side. A sign under the end gable reads: 'JR Mountey', who was the landlord here for a while. The stables were demolished and the stone used for extensions to the hotel, the work being carried out by J.W.Haynes of Belper. The hotel was modernised in 1965 by the Home Brewery. The 1968 *Historic and New Inns of Interest in Derbyshire* quoted the following: 'The hotel now has three very pleasant bars, the cocktail bar having a copper top and the lounge is tastefully finished in blue moquette with medium oak furniture. The very up to date dining room will seat 80 diners with comfort. All meals are a la carte and the menu comprehensive with an excellent stock of wines on hand, to regale customers who are made welcome in small or large numbers.' The hotel underwent further long overdue refurbishment in *c.*1990.

Derbyshire Yeomanry: This important sepia view by an unknown local photographer was taken in 1909 showing the 50 members of the Derbyshire Imperial Yeomanry passing through Ambergate, heading north to camp, possibly at Buxton. The two-horse-drawn delivery cart and driver, in leather apron, of W.E.Burrows Ltd stop to admire the cavalcade before completing their delivery of bottled Derby and Burton Ales to the Hurt Arms Hotel. Note the fine looking horse and cab parked outside the stables. These fine stables and the outbuildings to the rear are all lost, the area having been surfaced into an unusually and unnecessary large car park. The message on the reverse side recalls: 'Dear Florrie, I was with this trolley [*presume horse drawn*] when the Yeomanry came back from camp at the same place, this view must have been taken from the Platform of Ambergate Station, I think it is very good, Love Will.' Just beyond the stables, parallel with the main road, lies the old blacksmith's shop, whose smith travelled from Belper to work here. The stone steps to the right-hand end of the stables led to an upper room which Ambergate FC once used as changing rooms.

The Old Toll Bar at Ambergate: This originally sepia photograph from Blount's Real Photo Series of postcards issued *c.*1908 must be a reprint from a much earlier negative. It shows the old Toll House situated on a site at the junction of the Ripley and Matlock roads close to where today's Little Chef is situated. It was then titled 'The Amber Gate of the Cromford and Belper Turnpike Trust.' The junction of the turnpike from Nottingham with that from Belper to Cromford opened on 1 July 1818. The tollkeeper has just opened the tollgate to allow two horses and carts to travel northwards towards Matlock. Two of the round shaped stone pillars have been preserved and can be seen today at the entrance to Devonshire Street off Toadmoor Lane; and a further two are located near the old chapel situated close to the recreation ground. Ambergate FC once played in a field behind the viaduct on the right.

Matlock Road: In comparison with the previous view, this *c.*1930s view by Lilywhite Ltd, the postcard publishers from Halifax, shows clearly the changes that have taken place during 25 years. The Else Brothers Garage has been constructed close to the site of the former toll house, together with several new houses along the railway side of Matlock Road. Ambergate West Junction signal box stands on the right. The prestigious large house on the left, complete with turret and arched entrance, once belonged to Mr Kay, manager of the wire works. A policeman with white hat and gloves appears to be standing on point duty at the intersection of the Matlock and Ripley roads. Twigg's farmhouse on the canal bank is hidden behind the tree but the white appearance of their barn is clearly visible to the left of the tree. The large square-shaped Summersides, former residence of Thomas Summerside (an agent with the Clay Cross Co associated with Ambergate Lime Works), is visible in the distant right of the main road. The legendary George Stephenson is believed to have been resident here for a while.

Ambergate Floods: This scene, captured by a local amateur photographer, clearly shows the level of the flood water along the main Matlock Road (A6) and around the Hurt Arms Hotel in the winter of 1965. Corah's garage, selling Fina petrol, stands on the middle left and the new stone built public toilets on the right of the A610 Ripley Road corner. It was during these floods that locals Roy Hollingsworth and Ron Presley helped to rescue several sheep on Johnson's sports ground.

The derelict remains of the old Ambergate lime kilns can be seen in the background of this *c.*1965 black and white photograph (by Eric Green of Ambergate). The old traction engine is passing the open ground on the left and the former Esso Petroleum depot on the right. Ambergate Saw Mills (extreme right) were established here in 1856 by John Linacre. Today the site is home to the Ambergate Country Furniture business run by the Hudson family who have built up a prestigious reputation as craftsmen and now have a beautiful showroom here. The corrugated fencing around the building on the right is where old oil was stored for use as smokescreens in Derby during World War Two.

Gas processing plant: This later *c.*1966 photograph, again by Eric Green shows the new gas processing plant in its early state of construction. However, many other changes have taken place. The Staffordshire Farmers Ltd, have renovated the old shed belonging to Cowan's Transport and a new BP garage with petrol forecourt has opened up on the left side of the A610 Ripley Road. The new slip road has also been constructed (top right to the rear of the new gas plant). Some renovation work has also taken place to the buildings and yard on the near right of the A610. The stone building to the right of the Staffordshire Farmers at one time housed flats where well-known local Mr Bill Brocklehurst once resided.

Ripley Road: This view probably taken from platform 2 *c.*1967 shows the gas processing plant in an advanced stage of construction visible above the parapet of the railway bridge over the A610 Ripley Road. The large ornate stilted platform waiting room on the serviced platform 5 on the line to Matlock. This bridge was wide in 1876 by the addition of wrought-iron girders to carry the platf

the new triangular station. This bridge was demolished in 1985. large stone house and outbuilding on the right is believed to e initially belonged to Francis Hurt and later acquired by Joseph Glossop who had the nearby wood turning works. At a later stage the railway purchased the house and a Mr Percy Wheeler, permanent way inspector, and family lived here for many years.

Belper Road: Although titled Belper Road, this 1904 Valentine Series scene should really say Derby Road. This scene was produced both in colour and black and white. It is not clear what is exactly happening, but the small gathering of children are watching a young boy, complete with hand cart with a large metal bowl inside it. He appears to be stirring the contents. The message on the reverse side reads: 'Dear M, Hope you and F are keeping well, the first two cottages on the left of picture are ours. Mrs Forwood standing at door, signed Jos.' It was sent to Mrs W.Briggs, Clyde Cottage, Gregory Street, Ilkeston. The Jos is obviously short for Joseph Briggs, who lived at Mossley Villas and was the manager of the Ambergate Wire Works. A Mrs Elizabeth Forwood was recorded in 1895 as owning apartments in Ambergate, whilst a Mr Forwood was a railway goods foreman.

Derby Road: This is a Lilywhite Ltd mid-1940s production looking north from the vicinity of the Recreation Ground. Several children on the left are close to Elliot's grocer's shop. The heavily ivy-clad rectory stands on the right. The grassed area beyond tells us that Dean Road has yet to be built. The home on the extreme right has had the bay window added and was at one time Hawley's, who baked on the premises. The adjacent cottages now have porches added.

Derby Road: Valentines produced this 1904 view looking south down Derby Road. This view was published in colour and black and white. The main road at this time was quite rough with grass verges and grass in the centre. On the side of their lean-to front porch, the White House pub on the left advertises accommodation for cyclists . The porch has long gone. The first house adjacent to the pub was at this time a shop; it was variously a draper's and then a toffee shop. The house on the opposite corner of Toadmoor Lane was at one time the sweet shop of Louise Taylor, and Birks the cobbler's once had a business here.

Matlock Road: Ten years after the previous view the main road is still largely unmade without pavements. Workmen have dug a channel to the last house on Derwent Terrace, presumably associated with the drains. The shop sign of Herbert Naylor is just visible on the right opposite the White House; he was the local cycle agent and dealer. Next (south) to Naylor's stood the butcher's shop of Arthur Worrall and a butcher's shop still exists today, run by K.Birch. Just beyond the cycle shop lies the entrance to the old Co-operative Society shop. This 1913 Kingsway Series view shows the public house has now taken on a Mock Tudor appearance and the sign states 'The White House Inn'. The landlord at this time was Frederick Green.

This view taken nearly 30 years after the previous picture shows the road improvements on the right-hand side, although the left-hand verge is still quite rough. The White House still sells Stretton's Fine Derby Ales and Stout, but the new sign simply reads 'White House'. Open top car CH 2184' is parked near the former sweet shop adjacent to the pub.

The Vicarage: This *c.*1906 view of Matlock Road clearly shows the grassed verges and rudimentary main road (now the A6). The large stone house on the right is the Vicarage. In 1912, *Kelly's Directory* listed this as follows: 'The living is a perpetual curacy, net annual value £235 with residence, in the gift of five trustees, and held since 1897 by the Revd Harry Eardley Field BA of Durham University. By 1928 *Kelly's* recorded: 'The living is a vicarage, gross yearly value of £320 with residence, in the gift of the Johnson family and held since 1928 by the [then] newly-appointed Revd William Marsh Repson of London University. In 1995 the incumbant is the popular Revd David Rymer.On the left behind the tree, almost opposite the young white smocked Edwardian girl, stands the old United Methodist Free Church (Bethel chapel). Rose Cottages are to the left of the Vicarage and further on stood Haywood's drapery shop.

Day's Tea Rooms: This late 1920s photograph from the Blount's Series shows the substantial timber construction of Joseph Day's Tea Rooms parallel with the main Matlock Road. In 1928 Joseph Day was listed as having a refreshment room only, but it is evident from the various enamel advertising signs for Pratts and Castrol Motor Oils that at this time he also offered service to motorists. Joseph Day was affectionately referred to by locals as 'Dinkie' Day. Within the tea rooms he kept a famous monkey, which the locals and many visitors came to love apart from when it stole their hats. Several local residents remember the day it escaped and climbed on to the roof of the ivy-clad St Anne's Church, seen here in the background, and rang the church bell. Day's Tea Rooms became a popular calling place for the many visitors travelling towards the Peak District. The long wooden tea rooms had to be demolished as part of the railway and road re-widening scheme. Halfpenny Bridge is visible to the left of the picture.

Promenade Garage and Cafe: After Dinkie Day had established his popular refreshment rooms and small garage came the Promenade Garage and Cafe built approximately on the same site as part of the road and rail widening scheme of 1931-32. The cost associated is believed to have been defrayed by the authority responsible for the rewidening scheme. The cafe also housed the successful promenade Family Stores. The garage was Art Deco style, with illuminated petrol pumps and advertisements displaying popular brand names of the period, *eg.* Esso Lube, Esso Ethyl. The enamel sign to the right of the entrance optimistically states that 'Craven A cigarettes will not effect your throat'! At this stage the garage did not contain any workshops. The Rogers family kept the garage and stores for many years. This view also shows the house and bungalow now built in the space between the cafe and the church. The stores and cafe still exist today and offer good' friendly service from 'The Brummies' as the Newis family are known locally.

Mossley and Staly Villas: This early and rare view by an unknown local photographer shows how the ornate prestigious three-storey houses of Mossley and Staly Villas dominate the left-hand side of Derby Road. The curved retaining walls still look good today but underwent major re-strengthening during 1994. Former residents here were Bertram C.Barker and Joseph Briggs at Mossley and John Allsopp and Wallace Harber at Staly in 1912. Joseph Briggs was the former manager of the wire works, retiring to Mossley in 1910 where he became renowned for his violin repair work. W.W. Tunnicliffe, the first headmaster of Belper's Herbert Strutt School, was keen that music did not lag behind other activities and in May 1930 two cellos each costing £11 5s, together with a violin, were secured from Mrs Briggs of Ambergate. The left-hand pathway leads to Rockhouse. Some inhabitants employed servants and to the left-hand side of Mossley Villas, stone steps leading to the rear of the house were built so they could enter by the rear. The Villas were built by two brothers from Blackpool who saw the suitable plot of land when passing on the train. The first house, south of Staly Villas just in view, is rather oddly named Riverside and was the long-time former residence of Henry Peach who was a local artist. The message on the reverse of this card reads: 'Dear Lil, I have just arrived here cycling and half roasted.' It was posted on 9 July 1904.

The Bungalows: This mid-1940s scene shows the various housing along New Bridge Road and the new bungalows built along the hillside in the upper middle. Reference on the reverse side of this card is made to 'Seymour House on Newbridge Road standing quite on its own with no neighbours, so nice and private'. Ambergate [mixed] School, also in this view to the right, was erected in 1898 for 153 children; the average attendance in 1912, when John Joseph Kirk was the master and Miss C.Holmes the infants mistress, was 118 . The old Wesleyan Chapel is just visible in the extreme left with the rear of the large Promenade Cafe and Stores below.

The village: This general 1930s view by Frank Scarratt of Derby shows the old second station buildings on the left with Old Toadmoor now hidden in the array of new houses built in the previous 30 years on the hillside of Ambergate. Many large houses were sited on Newbridge Road, such as Fairfield, Newbridge House and Fernleigh. West Mount, the former home of Henry C.Sergeant, and Overdale House, the former home of Henry Shallcross, are here.

General view (West Bank): This illustration was published by the Kingsway Photo Series *c.*1914 and was sold at the W.H.Smith & Son stall on Ambergate station. The near and far lanes leading to West Bank are clearly visible. The square flat-roofed grocer's shop of John Henry Stone stands to the right at Woodend, on the main Derby Road. Mrs Mary Caroline Stone was the shopkeeper here in 1928. Arthur Kent had a boot repairer's business in the left-hand side of this building in 1912. To create the near lane to West Bank, a fairly large house, pictured on page 170, was demolished.

West Bank: This superb 1907 close-up view of West Bank by an unknown local photographer was taken from a high point (probably a tree) and clearly shows why the castellated flat-roof grocers of J.H.Stone has an address of Woodend, Ambergate. The house behind the shop was that of Woodside House, the home in 1895 of William Henry Stone. The simple message to the rear of the card reads: 'How do you like this view of my beloved West Bank and the woods? Love Ruth.' John Smith, the Midland Railway inspector, lived at West Bank. Stone's grocer's eventually became that of Spencer Wibberley, with Charles Smith, boot and shoe repairers, on the left-hand side of the shop. He was also the local postman. Behind the large house standing to the left of the first entrance lane to West Bank stands local butcher's Arthur Worrall's slaughter house which was later used by a fish and chip dealer on the Recreation Ground for stores and cutting his chips.

This general view by Valentines was part of their 1904 series, produced in colour and black and white. Mossley and Staly Villas stand on the main Derby Road (left) with the large house with left-hand front gable called Rockhouse set back higher to the left. A Mrs Jackson resided here for many years. A one-time occupant used to make his children walk barefoot in the summer to harden their feet. The 1898 school stands in the extreme upper left. The rear of Derwent Terraces are in the lower right. This scene shows how the former farmland between Derby Road and Toadmoor Lane has disappeared with many different types of housing being erected in the space of seven years.

General view: This Kingsway Series photograph of *c.*1914 shows an accurate recording of the rear of Derwent Terraces on the main Matlock Road opposite the White House. To the right of Derwent Terrace stands the old Co-operative Society shop, opened as a Ripley branch in 1899, with its arched rear window. This shop and the adjoining house, named Derwent House, were built by the Elliot family who originally had their general groceries business here prior to the Co-op. In 1928 Fred Hodgkinson lived in Derwent House. The row of houses at right angles on the other side of Derby Road are the stone houses of Devonshire Street. Many larger houses have also appeared on the upper portion of Newbridge Road.

Ambergate greetings: This five way multi-view publication by F.Frith & Co Ltd appears to be early 1940s and shows, among others images, the canal, toll house and St Anne's. The top right view shows the new houses built at Woodend to the right of the flat-roofed former grocer's shop of Wibberley's. The centre view shows the former garage belonging to the Swains, who also owned the adjacent house on Matlock Road.

The Old Post Office: Mail gig driver Mr Wain on board his horse-drawn carriage is captured in this Valentine Series featuring the original old Post Office in 1906. The sub-postmaster at the time was Isaac Adams, and previously had been Henry Adams. The Post Office also contained a grocery and drapery business during the late 1890s through to 1912. The old Post Office was eventually demolished so that the Matlock and Derby Road traffic could travel through separate bridge arches instead of the single arch as seen in this view.

Rear of old Post Office: Mrs Adams and friend stand on their balcony to the rear of the old Post Office peering towards the Valentine Co photographer situated on the opposite bank of the river. The Post and Money Order Office and Savings Bank at Ambergate received letters from Derby via Belper by mail gig, in 1878 arriving at 5.26am, dispatched at 7.30pm.

Post Office: Francis Scarratt, the 'people's photographer' from Derby, took this mid-1930s view of Ambergate's second Post Office. Mrs Annie Wilkins, postmistress, can be seen in the doorway which at this time faced on to Devonshire Street. A young girl is skipping on the pavement close to the Post Office which also contained a grocery business. The window display would suggest that towels and linen were also available here. The black and white half-timbered White House public house is on the lower right-hand side of Toadmoor Lane. The preserved former Matlock Road toll gate pillars stand at the entrance to Devonshire Street.

The village: F.Frith & Co of Reigate published this post-war view of the small portion of Ambergate village situated on either side of the main Matlock Road (A6). The new (and third) Post Office is situated on the left. The first family here were the Timperley's. Prior to being a Post Office it was for a while Petts Electrical shop. The former United Methodist Free Church is on the left, opposite the vicarage.

Ambergate FC: This fine team picture was taken by an unknown local photographer and shows Ambergate Football Club in the 1910-11 season. Five out of the 11 players were wearing neck scarves. Known names are, back row (left to right): second along Mr Willmot, third and fourth in line Charlie and Tom Varney, eighth Mr Shellcross and ninth Charlie Murphy.

Ambergate FC: This team photograph was taken at the front of the White House public house and shows Ambergate FC in the 1958-59 season when they won the Cavendish Cup. Team members are, back row (left to right): Unknown, Fred Blount, Glyn Martin, Mason, David Coope, Gerald Gibson. Middle row: Unknown, Ernie Wragg, Denis Watson, Henry Mason, Unknown. Front row: Tibby Parker, Unknown, Alf Sulley, Evans. Fred Blount, on the back row with white shirt, was at this time the landlord of the White House.

Main Road and Church: This *c.*1950 view shows St Anne's viewed from the railway. The old timbered cricket pavilion can be seen erected adjacent to the main road. The wall at the church end along Holly Lane has been whitened to form a sight-screen. The cricket ground was part of the Hurt Estate until the 1920s. In 1939 the owner, Mr Woodhouse, sold the land to the Home Brewery Co Ltd. Ambergate station signal box stands to the left.

Ambergate Show: The Ambergate Annual Flower Show and Sports was a well-attended event as shown in this *c.*1910 photograph by an unknown local photographer. The event was one of the largest in England. The Johnson family of Oakhurst ensured that this day was the social highlight of the year. Johnsons supplied the wood for spectators' seats and runners and cyclists came from near and far to compete. The prizes given by the Johnsons were highly coveted. During the show's early years few Ambergate inhabitants could afford summer holidays away from their homes and, as such, the Flower Show increased in importance. This scarce view shows that the show was held on the ground near the present Johnson & Nephew's Social Club and the former Chase Farm. A huge marquee has been erected left, together with a smaller one on the right. There were many side shows, swings and steam-driven merry-go-rounds. Many Midland Railway wagons are evident on the line to Whatstandwell, and Ambergate West Junction signal box stands on the right. George Stephenson's lime kilns are visible in the top right. In November 1919, the Johnsons held a victory sports and celebrations which included obstacle races and ladies' tug of war. After an enormous tea and the presentation of prizes, entertainment was provided, the highlight of the Grand Concert including a ventriloquist. The annual Ambergate Carnival is still a spectacle, being organised by an enthusiastic and inovative committee of locals. The carnival is now held on the Recreation Ground. Enthusiastic Ambergate horticulturists such as Sid Green, Eric Burton, Bert Taylor and John Hall, Cuth Wain and, to a lesser extent, Brian Smith and many others, still compete with one anther in fierce annual competition, and then auction their exhibits at the White House hostelry afterwards.

Carnival parade: This *c.*1930 Ambergate Carnival parade features several decorated floats each with many children on board as they slowly make their way to the Sports Ground in their horse-drawn floats. This photograph belongs to Mrs Rogers of Derby Road, Ambergate. The leading horse is level with Ambergate's first Post Office on the immediate right with the roof of the outbuilding in the bottom corner. On the left-hand side is Post Wood.

Buckland Hollow (the Excavator): This view shows BXA 926B being lowered on to the roof of the Excavator public house near Buckland Hollow. The vehicle remained here from 1981 to *c.*1987 and was the propriety of J.C.Balls, construction and excavation engineers. They removed it after Mr & Mrs J.C.Balls sold the pub to Marstons Brewery.

Buckland Hollow: This was a hamlet pleasantly situated one mile north-east from Heage on the Cromford Canal and here was the extensive establishment of German Wheatcroft & Son, carriers to all parts of the kingdom. This rare photograph shows the old former Wesleyan Chapel built about 1840 by Dav Wheatcroft, then owner of the land, and purchased by t Wesleyens from principal landowner F.N.Smith in 1886. It sto within its own neatly laid-out grounds and was somewh

ınique in style, being lighted from the top by an octagonal lome. On the opposite side stood the lodge house to ?. N.Smith's residence, erected by Mr Wheatcroft about 1849. Jp on the high ground, some distance from Buckland Hollow, is Prospects farmhouse, a fine structure in the Swiss style. The chapel was demolished, unnecessarily, to allow road widening.

Cricket team: Ambergate's first cricket ground was probably across the river behind Glossop's old woodyard (later Dean's Haulage) on the Ripley Road, or it may have been in the field next to the River Amber at the foot of the Chase. It was moved to the Hurt Arms' ground *c.*1890 and there is photographic proof of the club playing here in 1892, during St Anne's Church topping-out ceremony. This important photograph shows a team of 12 with committee or supporters. Note the fine figure in the centre back row, complete with moustache and 'Boer War hat'. The photograph was taken outside the Hurt Arms Hotel, *c.*1890-92.

Bertie Johnson ('the Colonel') encouraged the local cricket team, continuing a tradition set by his father, Thewlis. The wire works employees would change shifts to allow the best cricketers to represent Ambergate CC. The club's centenary was celebrated in 1985 when a brochure was published, mainly as a result of Lee Spendlove's hard work, with a foreword by the former Derbyshire skipper Derek Morgan. For every copy sold, 10p was donated to Ridgeway Hospital.

Over the years Ambergate CC has boasted many loyal players, many of them from the same family, and some of those long-serving cricketers were George, Henry and Arthur Holmes, Fred, Allan, Stuart, Roy and David Piper, Herbert, John and Dick Mountney, Fred Beaumont, the Byards, Whittinghams, Hiltons and the Worralls. Beefy Bert Taylor of Longlands Villas was a powerful all-rounder who enjoyed his heyday in the 1950s. Today's long-serving Ambergate cricketers include John Bradley, Lee Spendlove and Kevin Allen.

Ambergate Area Annals

1792	Halfpenny Bridge constructed over River Derwent by Francis Hurt.
1794	Cromford Canal opened.
1818	(1 July) turnpike junction (toll house) opened at junction of Ripley and Matlock Roads.
1837	Chapel on Newbridge Road opened by Methodists.
	Toad Moor became Amber Gate.
1840	(11 May) North Midland Railway opened through Ambergate.
	Buckland Hollow Wesleyan Chapel opened.
	George Stephenson commissioned Incline Mineral Railway to Crich.
1841	Ambergate Lime Works (Clay Cross Co) opened.
1846	Ambergate's first station (north of Toadmoor Tunnel) opened.
	(November) Station renamed Ambergate.
1848	Oakhurst Mansion built by Francis Hurt
1849	The Manchester, Buxton, Matlock & Midland Junction Railway opened.
1856	Ambergate's steam saw mills built by John Linacre.

Hurt Arms: This is another fine early photograph by 'W.G.' taken in 1904. The rear of the Hurt Arms stables and outbuildings can be seen, together with the collection of wooden beer crates and barrels on the ground to the rear of the hotel. To the right stands the stilted wooden waiting room of platform 5. Chase Cottage is visible in the middle distance over the canal.

1863 (1 June) Ambergate's second station (south of Toadmoor Tunnel) opened.

1869 The United Methodist Free Church (Bethel Chapel) erected on Derby Road.

1872 John Thewlis Johnson moved into Oakhurst.

1876 (10 Dec) Ambergate's unique triangular and third railway station opened.
Thatched House Tavern closed and converted to three cottages.
Hurt Arms Hotel constructed by Francis Hurt.
(2 May) Richard Johnson and Nephew's Ambergate wire works opened.

1884 Ambergate Station iron footbridge built by Smedley Bros.

1892 St Anne's Church opened and funded by John Thewlis Johnson.

1894 St Anne's redecorated and organ installed.

1895 John Thewlis Johnson died.

1898 Ambergate [mixed] School erected on Toadmoor Lane.

1899 Ambergate Co-operative shop (Ripley branch) opened on Matlock Road.

Francis Malcolm Stevenson  James Francis Stevenson

1907 (June) Derwent Valley Water Board began work on underground reservoirs.
Stevenson's early dye works in production at Bull Bridge.

1911 (July) Derwent Valley Water Board completed reservoir works.
Railway strike.

1924 (7 Nov) Oakhurst dedicated by Bishop of Southwell as Diocesan Retreat House.

1928-9 Longland Tunnel opened out into railway cutting.

1928-32 Ambergate Railway widening scheme and South Junction re-aligned.

1931 Promenade Garage, Cafe and Stores built.

1939 Ambergate cricket ground sold to Home Brewery.

1943 Fire at wire works forced temporary closure.

1944 Cromford Canal upper portion closed by LMS Railway.

1957 Crich quarries closed.

1964 Toll house on Halfpenny Bridge demolished.

1965 Ambergate flood near Hurt Arms and area.
(2 Oct) Ambergate lime works closed.

1966 Ambergate lime kilns demolished.

1966/7 Ambergate gas processing plant commissioned.

1967 (6 March) Ambergate station lost its main line services.

1968 (1 Jan) Ambergate station became an unmanned halt.

Stevenson's original dye house.

1985 Bull Bridge Canal Aqueduct demolished. Skew Bridge carrying railway over Ripley Road demolished.

Ambergate Cricket Club's centenary year.

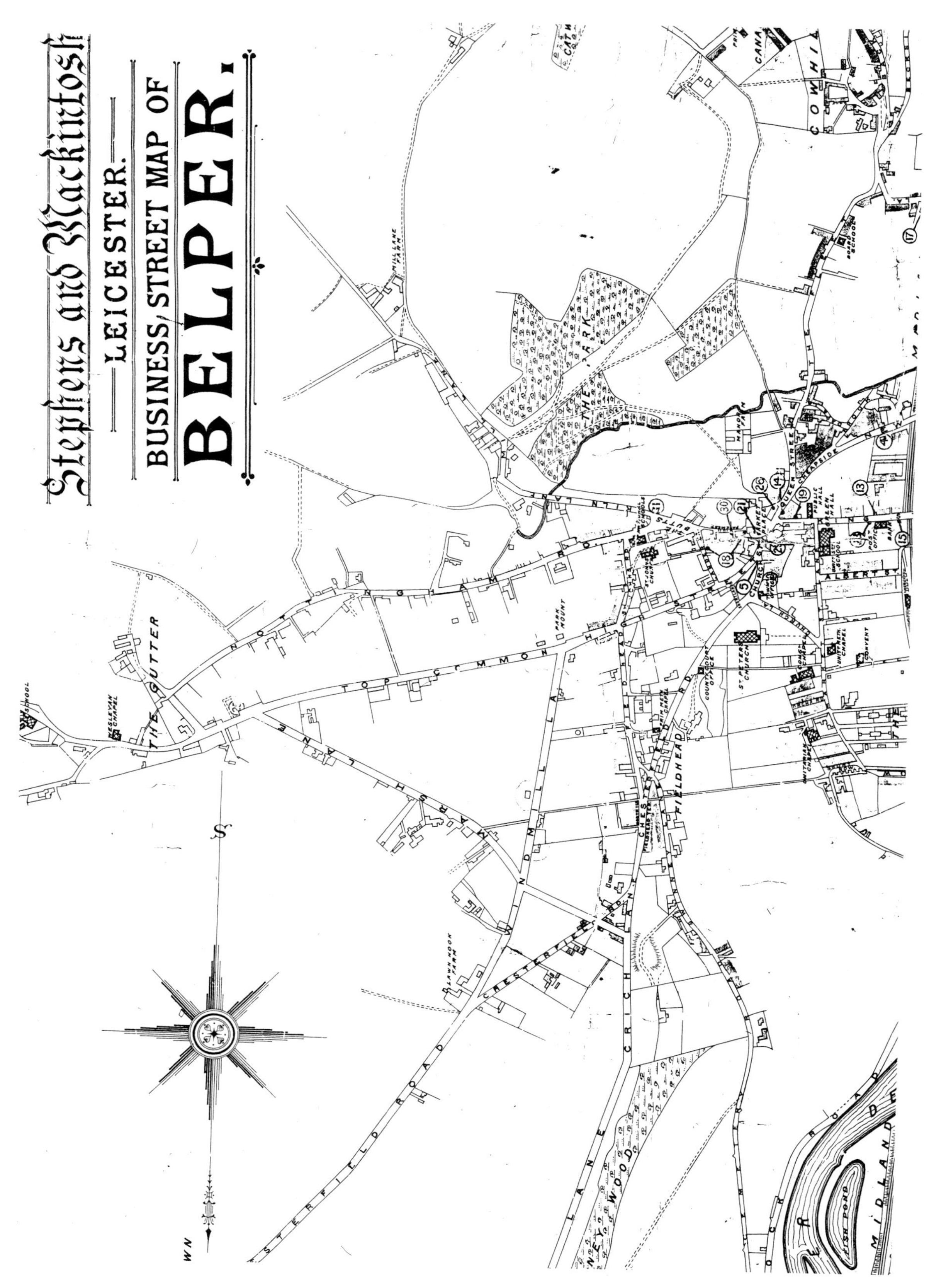

Extract from a map of Belper in the late 1890's by Stephens and Mackintosh

Belper Area Annals

1066	The De Ferrers family arrived after coming to England with William of Normandy.
1068	Belper recorded as 'Bradelei' in Domesday Book.
1250	St John's Chapel, near the Butts, believed to have been established.
1380	First wooden bridge built across the Derwent at Belper.
1609	Plague claimed 53 victims who were buried in the old Chapel Road.
1660	The Talbot Inn recorded.
1686	Thomas Bloomfield hanged at Derby for murder and his body gibbeted at Belper Dally.
1689	First Dissenting sect (Unitarian) in Belper.
1739	First market held in Belper.
	Football match played on the frozen River Derwent.
1740	Mr Christie was the first parson in Belper.
1760	Samuel Harrison, who for 25 years became Britain's leading tenor singer, was born in Belper.
1764	Dally Farm believed to have been built.
1765	Charles Burkin, who became a English champion boxer, born in Belper.
1770	Thomas Slater believed to have introduced Methodism to Belper.
1782	First Central Methodist Chapel (and Belper's second chapel) built on Chapel Street.
1786	John Wesley preached in Belper.
1789	Congregationalists came to Belper.
1795	Great flood destroyed Derwent Bridge.
1796-98	New Derwent Bridge constructed.
1796	Windmill erected in Belper by Synam of Heage.
1797	Far Laund toll gate demolished.
1801	Bull baiting in Belper Market Place.
1802	J.Mellor and J.Spencer, hanged for forgery, were interred in Chapel Yard.
1807	Second and larger Methodist Chapel opened in Chapel Street.
1813	Belper's first newspaper, The Derbyshire and Universal Weekly Advertiser printed and published by F.Mason.
1816	Pottery Wesleyan Chapel built.
1817	Primitive methodist Chapel, Field Head, erected.
1818	Savings Bank established at Belper.
1818-20	Baptist Chapel erected in Bridge Street.
1820	Cotton stacks burnt at Belper Mill.
1822	Duke of Devonshire laid first stone of St Peter's Church.
	Congregational Chapel, Green Bank, built.
1824	St Peter's Church dedicated.
	Belper Humane Society formed.
1828	Serious fire at Mason's Farm, Broadholme.
1834	High Street Infants' School established.
1835	George Brettle & Co's hosiery factory completed. George Brettle died.
1838-40	Union Workhouse, designed by Sir Gilbert Scott, built.
1840	Belper's first railway station (the North Midland) opened.
1841	Grammar School established on Chapel Street.
1843	Subscription Library established in the Public Hall.
1846	St Peter's licensed for celebration of marriages.
1849	Ward's warehouse damaged by fire.
	First single-storey National School (St Peter's) built on the Butts.
	Christ Church, Bridge Hill, erected.

	Belper Lane End Wesleyan Chapel and Sunday School built.
1850	James Mellor Pym established his wines and spirits business in Belper.
1852-53	Wellington Court houses built on Bridge Street.
1855	Smedley Brothers established their Eagle Ironworks on Becksitch Lane.
1856	United Free Methodist (Salem) Chapel built on Green Lane.
1857	Christ Church Vicarage built.
	Burial Board, consisting of nine members, formed.
1859	Belper Cemetery opened on Matlock Road.
1871	Bazaar held at Congregational Chapel School Room.
1872	New Congregational Chapel opened on Green Lane.
1877	Belper 'governed' by a local board.
1877-79	Belper Pottery School erected.
1877	Cow Hill School for Girls erected.
	High Street Infants' School taken over by School Board and enlarged in 1893.
1878	Belper's second railway station opened off King Street.
1881	Crompton & Evans Bank opened on King Street.
	Waterless Fountain erected in the Market Place.
1882	Fleet School for Boys built.
	New Public Hall erected in Upper King Street.
1885	St Laurence's Convent erected.
	Lucerne Villa, Sherwood Villa and the Ferns Houses built on Derby Road by John Smedley.
1886	Lady Well demolished by local waterworks company and reservoir formed.
	Ebeneezer Arthur Smedley donated organ to Congregational Church.
1887	Jubilee Hall in New Road built by Mrs Alfred Smedley.
1889-90	Babbington Hospital created around old workhouse by Wheeldon Brothers.
1890	Pottery School enlarged.
	Belper Lane End Chapel of St Faith's built.
	Beecholme College established off Green Lane.
1891	Windmill dismantled and irregular-shaped house created.
	St Mark's Mission Church, Openwoodgate, erected.
1892	Horse Society established at Belper.
	Town and Trade Association formed.
1893	Baptist Chapel rebuilt on Bridge Street.
1894	Belper Urban District Council formed.
1895	Belper Joint Hospital Committee formed.
	Long Row School enlarged.
1898	Park Foundry established on Derby Road.
1905	William Holden's workshops in Field Lane destroyed by fire.
	Pontoon bridge erected to serve sewage works and west side of River Derwent.
1907	Watergates and The Rise houses built on Ashbourne Road for Pym family.
1910-11	Two-storey National School (St John's) built on the Butts.
1911	Widening of High Pavement carried out.
1912	The massive red-brick East Mill built by the English Sewing Co.
1913	St Swithun's Mission, Holbrook Road, Cow Hill, built by Mrs Hanson.
1919	Roman Catholic Church dedicated to Our Lady of Perpetual Succour built with Priest House on Gibfield Lane (enlarged in 1989).
1934	Glow Worm factory established on Derby Road.
1959-60	Derwent Bridge widened.
1964	Brettles Factory sold to Courtaulds Ltd.